EXTREME CAKEOVERS

RICK AND SASHA REICHART

EXTREME CAKEOVERS

make showstopping desserts
from store-bought ingredients

CLARKSON POTTER/PUBLISHERS
NEW YORK

Published in the United States by Clarkson Potter/Publishers, an imprint of
the Crown Publishing Group, a division of Random House, Inc., New York.
www.crownpublishing.com
www.clarksonpotter.com

CLARKSON POTTER is a trademark and POTTER with
colophon is a registered trademark of Random House, Inc.

A Hollan Publishing, Inc., Concept

Library of Congress cataloging-in-publication data
Reichart, Rick.
  Extreme cakeovers / Rick and Sasha Reichart. — 1st ed.
    p. cm.
  Includes index.
1. Cake. I. Reichart, Sasha. II. Title.
  TX771.R45 2013
    641.86'53—dc23   2012024637

ISBN 978-0-307-98520-0
eISBN 978-0-307-98522-4

Printed in China

Book and cover design by Ashley Tucker
Book and cover photographs by Ryan Siphers

10 9 8 7 6 5 4 3 2 1

First Edition

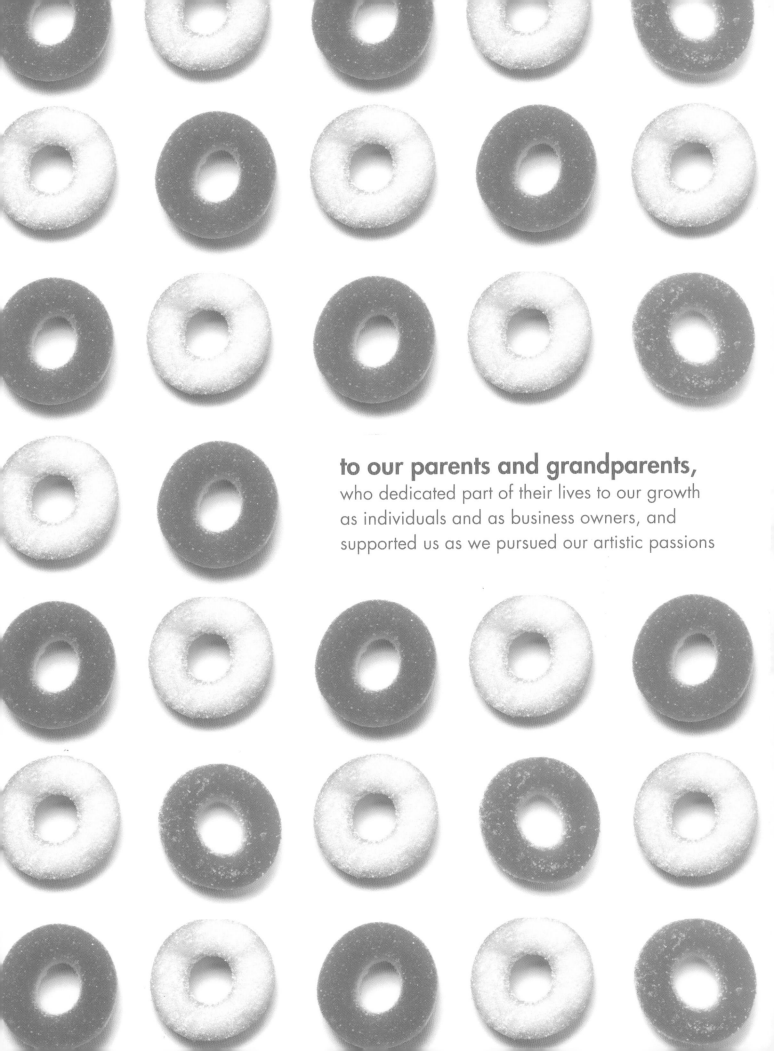

to our parents and grandparents,
who dedicated part of their lives to our growth
as individuals and as business owners, and
supported us as we pursued our artistic passions

contents

introduction

If you've ever looked at an intricate, showstopping, professionally decorated cake and thought, "I could never do that," this book is for you! No, we're not going to teach you how to execute a technically perfect tower of sugary goodness—but get ready to be amazed by the incredible cakes that anyone can construct using basic ingredients found in any grocery store.

In *Extreme Cakeovers,* we've made over ho-hum and even somewhat frighteningly decorated cakes that we picked up at our local store, transforming them into incredible creations that you'd be willing to bet came from some fancy cake shop and cost a pretty penny. With a little creativity—and a whole lot of different types of candy—you can craft a cool cake for any fun occasion.

As the owners of cakelava, our custom cake shop located in Kailua, Oahu, Hawaii, we have lots of experience being resourceful with baking and decorating techniques, not to mention executing crazy cakes that people dream up. We've made everything from a Marine helicopter to a giant gold Buddha—even a toilet bowl cake for a plumber. When we first opened in 2005, Rick, who had spent years decorating cakes in Los Angeles, found the Hawaiian humidity a shock. He had to adjust the way he made cakes to accommodate for the climate change, perfecting his handmade decorations using new ingredients and tweaking his methods. He put all of that resourcefulness to use in these designs, buying up all the candy we could find on our island to brainstorm clever ideas. While it's been a challenge in its own right, this book has been a blast to develop. Rick now sees Twinkies and Oreos in a new light, and I had a great time describing how to make red frosting look just like ketchup on our cheeseburger cake. We want the fun we have with the cakes to shine through.

We hope that this book will be a great resource for anyone who has the desire to make amazing cakes but feels limited by their lack of experience or creativity. We've done our best to remove the obstacles standing in the way of building an extravagant custom cake, while also making the process accessible and affordable. Even if you have never baked a cake, much less worked in a professional kitchen, you can still "make" a cake. Just purchase a sheet cake from the supermarket and we will show you how to turn it into a blank canvas with endless possibilities.

Rick has designed forty different cakes to choose from, and each one looks as if it could have come from a high-end cake shop. For the foodies, we have an entire chapter devoted to dinner foods. We have cakes just for girls and designs that guys of all ages will love. There are cakes that take you to exotic destinations and ones that take you back in time. There are cakes for children and techies and people who love zombies, and, of course, there are holiday cakes. There is a cake design to suit almost any celebration, or you can choose a cake and throw a party themed around it.

Each recipe reveals smart tricks of the trade that Rick has learned over the years. There are methods for frosting the cake smoothly, carving techniques to make three-dimensional designs, methods for adding structural support, and instructions for using food colors to paint on artful textures. You'll learn cake decorating terms like "crumb-coat" and how to turn an everyday zip-top plastic bag into an inexpensive decorating tool. While all of the projects call for store-bought cakes, if you prefer to bake from scratch, just turn to page 19 for our Basic Cake and Frosting recipes. The candies, cookies, and cakes used in this book are available in most grocery stores, candy stores, or baking and cake decorating supply stores, or they can be purchased on the internet. See the Sources section on page 201 for some of our favorite places to shop.

As you are making the cakes, be patient, especially when frosting the cake. Remember that you are new at this! Your decorating techniques will improve as you create more cakes, so don't get hung up on making a perfectly smooth surface or a precisely tinted blue frosting. Each cake has a noted level of difficulty to help you decide which is the best place to start, and to inspire you to make an advanced cake.

One of our favorite parts of putting the book together was working with all the candies—they're so much fun to play with! We want you to be creative with the goodies used on the cakes. Make substitutions, use ideas in our designs to create your own—do whatever you like. Cake decorating doesn't need to be serious or intimidating, and anyone can do it! Turn it into a family activity, or invite your friends over to spend a day in the kitchen creating the cake with you. You can show off your new cake decorating skills and then enjoy a slice together to celebrate your accomplishment.

happy caking!

tools and techniques

tools

All of the projects in this book are pretty simple. However, there are a few particular tools that will help make the job much easier. Here are our recommendations.

❶ small offset spatula: One of the most cherished tools in cake decorating, the small offset spatula, also called an elbow spatula, is used for spreading frosting, transferring cakes, crumb-coating, smoothing frosting, and making decorations. Its small size is perfect for frosting in hard-to-reach areas and gives more control than a large offset spatula when working with smaller surfaces.

❷ large offset spatula: The larger cousin of the small offset spatula, this handy tool has a blade averaging 6½ inches long and is perfect for frosting larger surfaces or transferring cakes or cookies.

❸ wooden skewers: Widely used in cake decorating for support and structure, wooden skewers come in a range of sizes.

❹ paintbrushes: Artist's paintbrushes can be a great tool for applying frosting or painting with food colorings. Purchase an inexpensive disposable set at a craft or art supply store.

❺ drinking straws: Disposable drinking straws are inserted into cakes to build structure and support.

❻ cake boards: Cake boards can be made out of any material that's strong enough to support the weight of the cake. See page 13 for a full range of options.

tip Sometimes it's a little tricky to add detailed decorations to the cakes. You may want to have on hand some clean tweezers to help you place candies more precisely.

❼ cardboard cake circles: Found in baking supply stores or craft stores, cardboard cake circles are sold in sets of varying sizes and are used to provide support underneath the cake.

❽ wire cutters: In cake decorating, wire cutters are used for cutting structural supports, such as wooden skewers.

❾ cloth- or paper-covered wires: Commonly found in craft stores and floral supply stores, cloth- or paper-covered wires come in a variety of colors and gauge sizes.

⑩ **toothpicks:** We use round, not flat, toothpicks throughout the book because round toothpicks insert smoothly into cake and are stronger than flat ones. Also, flat toothpicks can cause a candy to crack. Toothpicks provide light structural support and are also great for other small tasks, such as attaching candy decorations.

⑪ **pastry wheel / pizza cutter:** An everyday pizza cutter can stand in for a pastry wheel and is perfect for trimming rolled-out candy, cutting strips, or making shapes.

tip **Before you start a recipe, read through it once to become familiar with the ingredients, techniques, and steps. If you substitute an ingredient, choose a product that's similar in size, texture, and color for the best results. Measure and set out all ingredients in advance so that you can move efficiently through the project.**

⑫ **nonslip shelf liner:** Found in hardware stores and drugstores, nonslip shelf liner is used underneath rugs or on top of shelves to prevent glassware from slipping. We've found that a small piece is a perfect tool for adding decorative texture to a cake.

food colorings

We use three types of food coloring in this book: paste, gel paste, and liquid. They're each a little different, so we'll explain what they are and how to use them. There's also a powder food coloring, but we think it's hard to work with for these cakes and don't recommend it. The colorings can be found at baking supply stores, craft stores, and grocery stores.

❶ **paste:** Paste food coloring comes in a small cylindrical container and is very concentrated. It works well for tinting darker or more saturated colors, and it doesn't change the consistency of the frosting the way a liquid coloring can. This type of food coloring is more commonly found than the gel paste and can be purchased at kitchen supply stores and craft stores. To use it, insert a toothpick into the paste, and then swirl the toothpick into the frosting. Add small amounts of color at a time, each time using a fresh toothpick, until you get your

desired color. For a more saturated color, use the tip of a knife to dip into the color, making sure the knife is clean each time it is inserted into the jar. When tinting highly saturated colors like red, black, brown, royal blue, or green, it can take as much as 1 ounce of paste food coloring per cup of frosting.

❷ gel paste: More viscous than the paste colorings, gel paste comes in a squeeze bottle, so it is easy to dispense and less messy to use than paste. Gel paste is preferred over paste by cake decorating professionals because it's so easy to use. You can purchase gel paste at specialty baking or cake decorating supply stores. Gel paste colorings offer more intense and vibrant color options than liquid food colorings. Start with a drop or two for lighter colors, and for darker colors, add more gel paste until you achieve the desired shade. Like paste coloring, gel pastes are highly concentrated and won't water down your frosting.

❸ liquid: You can find liquid food coloring in any grocery store. Oftentimes we mix liquid food coloring with pure lemon extract for painting color onto candy. Pure lemon extract has a high amount of alcohol (about 85%) and evaporates quickly, so you end up with just the desired color. We do not recommend using liquid food coloring to tint the frostings because they are offer a weaker color than the gel or paste colorings and can water down the frosting.

cake boards

There are a few great cake board options that are available at baking supply stores, craft stores, and even grocery stores that have a baking section. Any of them work well, but throughout the book we have used painted ¼-inch-thick wood boards, which is what we use for the professional cakes we make. Painted wood boards allow you to customize the size and color of the board to each cake, and they lend extra support for the heaviest cakes. If you're comfortable with an electric saw—or have access to a hardware store or a Home Depot that will cut boards to order—and you're up for the extra work of painting, this is a great option. Note that the bottom of the cake should never come in contact with the painted board. Always first put the cake on a piece of cardboard. Some other great options include the following:

silver cake boards: These strong corrugated boards are grease-resistant and good for cakes that are not too heavy or structural. They come in a great variety of sizes.

tip **Start and finish a recipe on the same day so you don't have to refrigerate a partially completed cake overnight. In decorating, cakes are brought in and out of refrigeration to firm up the frosting. Leaving a decorated cake in the refrigerator overnight could cause the candies to melt and the frosting colors to bleed when the cake is pulled out of the refrigerator and into the warm air. If you want to chill the cake overnight while you are making it, frost the cake and then put the decorations on the next day after the cake has warmed up to room temperature.**

silver cake bases: Thicker than silver cake boards, silver cake bases usually run about ½-inch thick and are covered in grease-resistant paper. They are food-safe, reusable, and work well for cakes that require more support.

foam core covered in grease-resistant paper: Foam core is lightweight, quite strong as a support, and easy to cut to whatever size you desire; however, do not use it without first wrapping it in grease-resistant paper. We like Wilton's Fanci-Foil as a wrapping, and aluminum foil also works well.

techniques

Before you get started, read through these quick instructions for the best approach to these projects. Using the simple techniques outlined below, you'll end up with the most professional-looking cake.

removing decorations from a store-bought sheet cake

When you purchase a sheet cake from the grocery store bakery, it's likely already frosted and decorated with bright flowers, streamers, balloons, or other festive designs. You'll need to take off all of these layers before starting on one of the cakes in this book. This is a simple step, but take a moment to read through the following instructions so that you start off on the right foot.

tip If you are working in a cold, dry climate, fruit chews and Tootsie Rolls may be tough to work with. Put them in the microwave for a few seconds and they'll soften up. This will make it easier to shape and roll out the candies as needed. If you're working in a warm or humid climate, refrigerate frostings prior to using. They are easier to work with when they're firm.

Using a small offset spatula, remove the decorations on the top of the cake by gliding the back side of the spatula across the cake and scraping the frosting into a bowl. Start on one side of the cake and work toward the other side, removing the decorations layer by layer and preserving as much of the base frosting as possible.

Next, remove the frosting borders by scraping the back side of the offset spatula down each side of the cake. When working on the sides of the cake, be careful to scrape off only the excess frosting and not remove any of the actual cake. You want to preserve the shape of the cake, so be especially careful with the corners.

When all the decorations have been removed, add a new layer of fresh frosting—using a store-bought variety or one of the homemade ones on page 21—according to the instructions for the particular cake you are making.

tip Fix a saggy corner by building it up with an extra amount of buttercream. Apply the frosting to the corner and, using the backside of an offset spatula, smooth the side walls to make them even. Then smooth over the top of the corner.

trimming a cake board

All purchased cakes come on cake boards. We suggest that you trim the included cake board and then put the cake—and its board—on a new one, for a few reasons: For one, the cake boards found at baking supply or craft stores are more attractive than the boards that come with the cake. Also, the included board is usually not big enough or strong enough to properly support the cakes in this book. And, you won't be able to lift the cake off the board without potentially damaging it, so trimming the board now keeps your cake intact.

Pull the cake board just over the edge of your counter until the side of the cake is in line with the edge. Holding the board with one hand, and a chef's or serrated knife with the other hand, cut flush around the perimeter of the cake with a sawing motion. If it is easier, you can use scissors to trim the board. Repeat on all sides of the cake. Attach the cake and board to a new cake board with glue.

tip When stirring frosting, use a rubber spatula instead of a whisk to avoid introducing air into the frosting, creating unwanted bubbles. Aim to use the amount of frosting called for and no more. Sometimes beginners will use too much frosting, so try to frost lightly.

frosting 101

All the beautiful designs on top of these cakes need a great foundation. The frosting technique separates a skilled cake decorator from an amateur. Make sure to use the frosting sparingly and apply it to the cake with an offset spatula in smooth, long, even strokes. Short and choppy strokes will produce a frosting that looks messy and bumpy.

Start by crumb-coating the cake. A crumb coat is a thin layer of frosting that is applied to the cake with an offset spatula; it adheres to the crumbs and provides a clean surface for the final layer of frosting. Think of it as a primer before your main coat of frosting. Once the crumb coat is applied, allow it to firm up in the refrigerator before frosting the cake. Your second coat of frosting will be crumb-free and much smoother than if you had applied one coat alone.

After you apply your final coat of frosting, it is important to take the time to smooth it out using a small offset spatula. Simply run your offset spatula under hot water, give it a shake to remove the excess water, and while the spatula is still warm, carefully smooth the frosting. Remember to use even, long strokes to glide over the frosting. Repeat this procedure after each final coat of frosting for the best appearance.

using a zip-top plastic bag for piping frosting: A zip-top plastic bag is easier to use and more cost-effective than a pastry piping bag. Have a box of zip-top plastic bags on hand as you work through the recipes. We prefer the quart-size bags, because they can hold a good amount of frosting and still leave space at the top. Fill them with frosting as needed and cut the tip with scissors to create a variety of frosting decorations.

To fill the zip-top plastic bag, put the bottom of the bag in your hand and fold the top down over your wrist until about half of the bag covers your hand and forms a cup [photo 1]. Using a rubber spatula, spoon the frosting into the cup of your hand, scraping the spatula against the side of the bag as you fill it [photo 2]. Lift up the edges of the bag, squeezing the frosting down into the corner while you press out any excess air. Seal the bag. Once the bag is sealed, hold the bag and cut the tip with scissors according to the recipe instructions [photo 3].

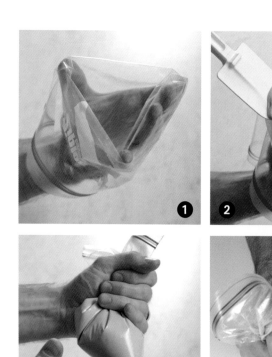

piping: Once the zip-top plastic bags have been filled with frosting, you can begin piping on the cakes. There are different ways to hold these bags depending on whether the piped lines run side-to-side or up and down.

To pipe lines running up and down, cup the bag with your thumb on the bottom side and your forefinger on the top, squeezing the frosting by applying pressure to the top of the bag. Using your other hand, place a finger on the bottom side near the tip of the bag to guide the frosting and steady the hand while piping.

tip Remember to breathe while piping icing! Breathing will help you make smooth lines and designs.

For lines running side-to-side, cup the bag with your palm facing outwards and gently squeeze the frosting by applying pressure at the top of the bag. Use the forefinger of your opposite hand to stabilize the piping hand [photo 4].

trimming a pound cake

Designs that are sculpted or carved into require a dense cake to work with. We use the Sara Lee frozen pound cake from the supermarket, as it holds its shape and is easy to cut. You can work with the pound cake either frozen or thawed. Just remember: At no point should the knife be pointed toward you. To trim the top of the pound cake, stand the cake on its side with the rounded side facing to the right if you are right-handed. Hold the cake with your left hand as you trim away the crust with the knife in your right hand. Trim away the crust on the sides in the same way, always cutting with the knife pointed away from you.

making a wedge cut: Sculpting a cake is one of the most difficult techniques in cake decorating. We have made it easier by utilizing a triangular wedge shape. The cake is measured and marked, and then the corners are cut with a knife following the markings. We've included a couple of examples for the wedge-cutting techniques for two cakes: the purse and the fire engine. Other cakes using the wedge cut have similar cutting techniques.

WEDGE TECHNIQUE FOR THE PURSE CAKE: Start at Step 2 (page 97) in the recipe, after the pound cakes have been stacked on top of each other. Cut equal amounts off the left and right sides of the stack to make it 8½ inches across [photo 1]. Using a knife, score two lines along the length of the top of the stack, one 1½ inches from the top edge and the other 1½ inches from the bottom edge [photo 2]. Stand the stack up on its short side with the scored lines facing you. Line up a knife on the top surface between the beginning of the left scored line and the top left corner on the same surface [photo 3]. Cut down following the scored line, and discard the cut-off piece. Then repeat on the right side [photos 4 and 5]. When you are finished, the cake should resemble a wedge with a flat top [photo 6].

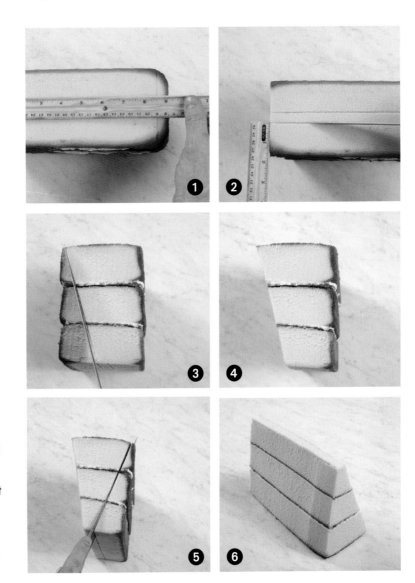

WEDGE TECHNIQUE FOR THE FIRE ENGINE CAKE: Start at Step 2 (page 57) in the recipe and place a second pound cake on a work surface horizontally. Using a knife, cut 4 inches off the right side, discarding the trimming [photo 1]. Flip the 4-inch piece on its side and cut its thickness in half, discarding one of the halves [photo 2]. Stack the 4-inch piece on top of the third pound cake, flush to one side, and attach it with a thin layer of frosting. Place the stacked cake vertically on a work surface with the thick end farthest away from you. Use a knife to score a line across the thick end 1½ inches below the top edge [photo 3]. Flip the cake on

its side with the scored line facing to the right. Line up a knife between the top left corner and the beginning of the scored line on the same surface, and then cut down following the scored line; discard the corner [photo 4]. Flip the cake back over, stack it on top of the pound cake that's on the 12-inch cardboard circle, and attach it with frosting [photo 5]. The cake should now resemble a fire engine.

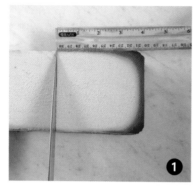
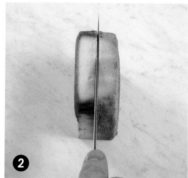

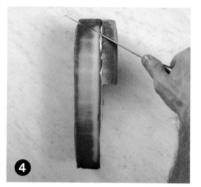

basic cake and frosting recipes

We use store-bought cakes and frostings throughout this book, which is helpful if you're short on time or aren't interested in baking from scratch. But if you love to bake or want your cakes to have a delicious homemade flavor, here are recipes for vanilla cake and chocolate cake, and for vanilla frosting and chocolate frosting.

The vanilla and chocolate frosting recipes will make a frosting that is more stable and easier to work with than the store-bought versions. Our homemade frosting has more body and will keep its shape better. Keep in mind that you should always crumb-coat the cake with the same frosting flavor as the final frosting you'll be using on the cake.

Each recipe has instructions for attaching the cardboard to the bottom of the freshly baked cake and for crumb-coating it with frosting. Then you're all set to begin!

vanilla cake

makes one 9 × 13-inch cake (¼ sheet cake)

1⅛ cups unsalted butter, softened

2¼ cups sugar

1¾ cups cake flour

1½ cups all-purpose flour

1 tablespoon baking powder

½ teaspoon salt

1¼ cups whole milk

2½ teaspoons pure vanilla extract

4 large eggs

1 can vanilla frosting, or 1½ to 2 cups homemade Vanilla Frosting (page 21), for crumb-coating

Preheat the oven to 350°F. Spray the bottom and sides of a 9 × 13-inch baking pan with nonstick cooking spray and line the bottom with parchment paper.

Put the butter and sugar in the bowl of a stand mixer fitted with the paddle attachment and beat on medium speed until light and fluffy, about 3 minutes.

In a large bowl, sift together both flours, the baking powder, and salt. In a separate bowl, combine the milk and vanilla.

With the mixer running on low speed, add the eggs to the butter mixture one at a time. Starting with the flour and working in two batches, add the flour mixture and the milk mixture alternately to the butter mixture. Scrape the sides of the bowl after each addition and beat until thoroughly combined. Then increase the speed to medium and beat for 20 seconds.

Pour the batter into the prepared baking pan. Bake for about 50 minutes, or until the top springs back when touched and a toothpick inserted in the center comes out clean. Transfer the pan to a wire rack and let the cake cool to room temperature.

Once the cake is cool, wrap it, still in the pan, in two layers of plastic wrap. Refrigerate it overnight; this ensures that it will be firm when you begin working with it. (The cake will keep for up to 7 days.)

When you're ready to begin working with the cake, take the cake out of the pan by running a metal spatula along the sides of the pan, flipping the cake onto a work

CONTINUES ➡

surface, and removing the pan and parchment paper. Flip the cake back over, and using a serrated knife, cut the top off so that it's flat. Flip the cake over again so you are viewing the bottom, and trim the edges so it measures 8 × 12 inches.

Attach the cake to a 9 × 13-inch piece of cardboard using a little frosting as "glue." Using a small offset spatula, crumb-coat the cake with a thin layer of vanilla frosting.

chocolate cake

makes one 9 × 13-inch cake (¼ sheet cake)

1 cup unsalted butter, softened

2 cups sugar

2¾ cups all-purpose flour

1⅓ cups unsweetened cocoa powder

2 teaspoons baking powder

1¼ teaspoons baking soda

1 teaspoon salt

2 cups whole milk

2 teaspoons pure vanilla extract

1 tablespoon instant coffee granules

2 large eggs

1¼ cups sour cream

1 can chocolate frosting, or 1¾ cups homemade Chocolate Frosting (page 21), for crumb-coating

Preheat the oven to 350°F. Spray the bottom and sides of a 9 × 13-inch baking pan with nonstick cooking spray and line the bottom with parchment paper.

Put the butter and sugar in the bowl of a stand mixer fitted with the paddle attachment and beat on medium speed until light and fluffy, about 3 minutes.

In a large bowl, sift together the flour, cocoa powder, baking powder, baking soda, and salt. In a separate bowl, whisk together the milk, vanilla, and instant coffee granules until the coffee is dissolved.

With the mixer running on low speed, add the eggs to the butter mixture one at a time. Add the sour cream and beat until combined. Starting with the flour and working in two batches, add the flour mixture and the milk mixture alternately to the butter mixture. Scrape the sides of the bowl after each addition and beat until combined. Then increase the mixer speed to medium and beat for 20 seconds.

tip If a cake design recipe calls for a half sheet instead of a quarter sheet, you can place two 8 × 12-inch cakes side by side on a 13 × 17-inch piece of cardboard. Use 1½ to 2 cans of chocolate frosting or 2¾ to 3½ cups homemade frosting to crumb-coat.

Pour the batter into the prepared baking pan. Bake for about 55 minutes, or until the top springs back when touched and a toothpick inserted in the center comes out clean. Transfer the baking pan to a wire rack and let the cake cool to room temperature.

Once the cake is cool, wrap it—still in the pan—in two layers of plastic wrap. Refrigerate it overnight; this ensures that it will be firm when you begin working with it. (The cake will keep for up to 7 days.)

When you're ready to begin working with the cake, take the cake out of the pan by running a metal spatula along the sides of the pan, flipping the cake out onto the work surface, and removing the pan and parchment paper. Flip the cake back over, and using a serrated knife, cut the top off so that it's flat. Flip the cake over again so you are viewing the bottom, and trim the edges so it measures 8 × 12 inches.

Attach the cake to a 9 × 13-inch piece of cardboard using a little frosting as "glue." Using a small offset spatula, crumb-coat the cake with a thin layer of chocolate frosting.

vanilla frosting

makes 2¾ cups (the equivalent of about 1¾ 16-ounce cans)

1⅓ cups unsalted butter, softened
½ cup solid vegetable shortening
1½ cups powdered sugar

¼ teaspoon salt
2 tablespoons hot water
1 teaspoon pure vanilla extract

Put the butter and shortening in the bowl of a stand mixer fitted with the paddle attachment and beat on medium speed until smooth, 2 to 3 minutes.

In a separate bowl, sift together the powdered sugar and salt. Add the hot water and vanilla, and whisk to make a smooth paste.

Turn the mixer to low speed and add the powdered sugar mixture. Mix for 3 to 4 minutes until thoroughly combined and smooth. Use immediately, or store in an airtight container in the refrigerator for up to a month.

chocolate frosting

makes 3½ cups (the equivalent of about 2 16-ounce cans)

½ cup unsalted butter, softened
1 (8-ounce) package cream cheese
4 cups powdered sugar

¾ cup unsweetened cocoa powder
2 tablespoons warm water

Put the butter and cream cheese in the bowl of a stand mixer fitted with the paddle attachment and beat on medium speed until smooth, 2 to 3 minutes.

In a separate bowl, sift together the powdered sugar and cocoa powder.

With the mixer running on low speed and working in two batches, add the sugar mixture and the warm water alternately to the butter mixture. Beat for about 1 minute or until smooth. Use immediately, or store in an airtight container in the refrigerator until the use-by date on the cream cheese expires.

dinner
IS SERVED

cheeseburger and french fries

We grew up having backyard barbecues at home, with big juicy burgers piled with crisp lettuce, tomatoes, pickles, and melted cheese. Served with french fries, the combination is unbeatable. When developing this recipe, we discovered that Cocoa Pebbles Treats make a very realistic patty. As the burger was assembled and ketchup squeezed on the fries, we started planning a trip to our favorite burger joint.

SERVES 2 TO 4

LEVEL OF DIFFICULTY: 2

special tools

Small offset spatula

1 **red plastic deli basket** (SEE SOURCES, PAGE 201)

1 **(10 × 10-inch) piece parchment paper**

ingredients

2 **bakery glazed doughnuts (about 4 inches in diameter)**

4 **Betty Crocker Blastin' Berry Hot Colors Fruit Roll-ups in Blazin' Blue/Green (green is used)**

2 **Betty Crocker Blastin' Berry Hot Colors Fruit Roll-ups in Sizzlin' Red/Yellow (yellow is used)**

1½ **cups vanilla frosting (1 16-ounce can)**

¼ **cup plus 2 tablespoons chocolate frosting (from 1 16-ounce can)**

Liquid food coloring: yellow and red

½ **teaspoon white sesame seeds**

Cornstarch, for dusting

5 **(.77-ounce) packages Cocoa Pebbles Treats**

4 **Haribo Wheels, strawberry flavor**

2 **green Sunkist Fruit Gems**

1 **(16-ounce) frozen pound cake (we use Sara Lee family-size), thawed**

1 to prepare

Refrigerate the doughnuts for 10 to 15 minutes and the 6 fruit roll-ups for at least 3 minutes. It's best to work with them when they're firm.

2 make the bun

To make the bottom half of the bun, using a serrated knife, slice off one fourth of the top of one doughnut. For the top bun, slice off one fourth of the bottom (i.e., the flatter side) of the second doughnut and use the trimmings to fill in the hole, making it as level as possible. Put the top and bottom doughnut buns on separate plates, facing the bottom bun cut side up and the top bun cut side down to preserve their shape.

The realistic look of the bun is achieved by layering three different shades of brown frosting with varying amounts of coverage, and refrigerating between frostings. In a small bowl, mix ½ cup vanilla frosting with 1 teaspoon chocolate frosting and 3 drops yellow food coloring. Using a small offset spatula, frost the top bun to fully cover it. Shape the bun by running the back side of the spatula from bottom to top, working around it. Dip the spatula in hot water, shake off the excess, and smooth the frosting. Refrigerate the top bun. For the bottom bun, frost just the sides. Smooth the frosting in the same manner, and refrigerate until the frosting is firm.

In this same bowl of frosting, add 1 drop red food coloring, 6 drops yellow food coloring, and ½ teaspoon chocolate frosting to make a golden-beige color.

Retrieve the top bun from the refrigerator. Frost a thin layer of golden-beige, but this time, use random strokes for a painterly look, placing emphasis on the top of the bun and being careful not to cover the entire thing. Smooth the frosting in the previous manner, and refrigerate. Repeat with the bottom bun. Set the frosting aside.

In a clean bowl, mix 2 teaspoons chocolate frosting with 2 teaspoons vanilla frosting. Take the top bun from the refrigerator and frost a thin layer with the new color as you did in the last step, focusing on the top portion. Sprinkle ½ teaspoon of the sesame seeds over the top of the bun, and refrigerate. Repeat the frosting on the bottom bun, but do not sprinkle with sesame seeds. Set aside but do not refrigerate.

3 make the lettuce

Dust the work surface with cornstarch. Remove 4 blue-green fruit roll-ups from the refrigerator and wait 15 to 30 seconds for them to become more pliable. Unravel them and cut off the green side, discarding the blue. Take a piece in your hand and make a loose, wavy shape by bending and stretching the wide side of the fruit roll. Put it on the bottom bun, hanging over the edge. Repeat with the remaining 3 pieces of green roll-up until the bottom bun is completely covered.

4 make the patty and cheese

Using your hands, smash all the Cocoa Pebbles Treats together and mix well. Roll the mixture into a ball, and press it into a burger patty. The patty should be slightly larger than the bun but not hide the lettuce. Put the patty on the lettuce.

Add more cornstarch to your work surface, if necessary. Remove 2 red/yellow fruit roll-ups from the refrigerator and wait 15 to 30 seconds for them to become more pliable. Unravel them and cut out the yellow parts to make the cheese. Overlap them slightly, and position them on the burger patty.

5 make the tomatoes, pickles, and ketchup

Take the 4 strawberry wheels and space them evenly on the cheese, close to the edge of the burger. For the pickles, cut the 2 green Sunkist Fruit Gems in half and insert them between the tomatoes, attaching them with a small amount of chocolate frosting.

In a small microwave-safe bowl, mix the reserved frosting from frosting the bun with red food coloring to create the ketchup. If necessary, add more frosting to make ¼ cup. Microwave for 7 to 10 seconds or until melted, and stir with an offset spatula. Carefully pour a small amount of ketchup near the edge of the burger patty, letting it ooze down the side. Set the remaining ketchup aside.

Remove the top bun from the refrigerator and attach it to the burger with 1 tablespoon of chocolate frosting, placed in the center. Refrigerate the whole burger until the frosting on the bottom bun is firm, 15 to 20 minutes.

6 make the french fries

Using a chef's knife, remove the top crust of the pound cake to completely level it. Then cut off enough of the top of the cake to make the bottom portion 1 inch thick; discard the top piece. Place the cake horizontally and cut it, crust side down, crosswise into ½-inch-wide strips; cut the thickness of each strip in half. Each piece should now be ½ inch square and resemble a french fry. There will be extra french fries if one breaks.

7 prepare the basket

Hold the piece of parchment paper by its diagonal corners and press it into the basket. Attach the paper to the bottom of the basket with a small piece of masking tape.

8 finish the cake

Using your hand and an offset spatula, put the burger in one side of the basket. To make the burger level, use the spatula to lift the front of it and position 2 french fries underneath. Pile the french fries next to the burger. Melt the ketchup frosting again and pour it over the fries.

taco plate

Tacos are a bit of an obsession for us. One year for Rick's birthday, our family surprised him with a custom taco plate cake, and it remains one of his most cherished birthday memories. For this cake, we wanted to capture the different textures found in the food and to find something that looked like a corn tortilla. The frozen waffle with the ridges cut off worked beautifully!

SERVES 20 TO 25

LEVEL OF DIFFICULTY: 3

special tools

- 1 (9 × 13-inch) cake board
  Small offset spatula
- 2 (5 × 5-inch) pieces corrugated cardboard
- 2 (5 × 5-inch) pieces parchment paper
- ½-inch flat-head paintbrush
- #4 round artist's paintbrush

ingredients

- 1 (8 × 12-inch) sheet cake (¼ sheet) with vanilla frosting
- 3¾ cups vanilla frosting (2½ 16-ounce cans)
- 2 frozen Eggo Buttermilk Waffles, thawed
- 10 round vanilla wafers, finely ground
- ½ cup chocolate melting wafers (SEE SOURCES, PAGE 201)
- 6 (.77-ounce) Cocoa Pebbles Treats
- ¾ cup chocolate frosting (from 1 16-ounce can)
- 3 marshmallows
  Cornstarch, for dusting
- 2 Betty Crocker Blastin' Berry Hot Colors Fruit Roll-ups in Blazin' Blue/Green
- 14 jujubes: 12 red and 2 green
- 2 Twizzlers, Rainbow flavors: 1 yellow and 1 green
- 2 individual chocolate pudding cups
- 2 (1.58-ounce) packages Raisinets
- ⅓ cup Rice Krispies cereal
- 1 individual vanilla pudding cup
  Paste or gel paste food coloring: green and yellow (SEE SOURCES, PAGE 201)

❶ make the taco platter

Remove the frosting decorations from the cake and trim the cake board (see pages 14 and 15). Measure 1½ inches diagonally from each corner toward the center of the cake, and then cut off the corners to round the cake into an oval. Using scissors, cut away the exposed cardboard corners underneath. Put the cake on a cake board and attach it with glue.

In a medium bowl, stir ½ cup vanilla frosting until smooth. Using a small offset spatula, crumb-coat the cake with a thin layer of frosting (see page 15). Refrigerate until firm, about 30 minutes.

Next, stir 2 cups vanilla frosting until smooth. Frost the cake completely, smoothing and rounding the corners. Clean up the board, and refrigerate the cake. Reserve the leftover vanilla frosting.

❷ make the tacos

Using a serrated knife, carefully cut away the ridges on both sides of the waffles, cutting as close as possible to the interior of the waffle without breaking it. The grid pattern will still be visible, but most of the ridges will be gone.

Using an offset spatula, cover one side of each waffle with a thin layer of vanilla frosting. Sprinkle the ground wafers over the frosting, carefully patting them down and brushing off any excess crumbs. Gently put the 2 taco tortillas on a work surface, crumb side up.

To create molds for the taco shells, make a tent with each of the corrugated cardboard squares by folding it in half, leaving a 2-inch gap. Put a piece of masking tape across the sides to hold the tent open. Place the tents, folded side up, on a plate or baking sheet. Fold each of the parchment squares in half, and lay one on top of each cardboard tent.

In a microwave-safe bowl, melt the chocolate wafers at 10-second intervals, stirring as needed, until fully melted. Hold a waffle tortilla crumb side down in your palm. With the flat-head paintbrush, brush the top with the melted chocolate. Then center the waffle tortilla, chocolate side down, on top of the parchment-covered tent. Repeat with the other waffle tortilla. Refrigerate until the taco meat wedges are completed, in the next step. Wash and dry the paintbrush.

❸ make the taco meat

Using your hands, smash together 3 of the Cocoa Pebbles Treats and form a half-circle wedge that's about 4½ inches long and 2 inches thick. The wedge should be thinner on the bottom and thicker on top to fill the shell. Repeat with the remaining 3 treats, and set the meat wedges aside.

Hold one taco shell upside down in your palm. Gently remove the cardboard tent and peel away the parchment paper. Dip the flat-head paintbrush into chocolate frosting, brush it on the inside of the taco shell, and insert one of the meat wedges. Gently press the taco shell together to bind the meat to the shell. Set aside, propping it up with a marshmallow on each side, but do not refrigerate. Repeat with the second taco.

4 add the taco toppings

Dust a work surface with cornstarch. Unwrap 1 blue/green fruit roll-up and cut out the green part. Slice it into ¼-inch-wide strips to make the shredded lettuce. Put the lettuce on the tacos.

To make the tomato topping, cut 8 red jujubes in half and divide them between the tacos, using water and a #4 paintbrush to attach them.

To make the cheese, cut half a yellow Twizzler into thin diagonal slices, then in half lengthwise. Sprinkle most of the cheese over the tacos, setting some aside for the refried beans. Attach the cheese to the tacos with water and a #4 paintbrush. Refrigerate the tacos for no more than 15 minutes.

5 decorate the platter

In a small bowl, stir ½ cup vanilla frosting until smooth, and spoon it into a zip-top plastic bag. Cut ½ inch off the tip with scissors, and pipe a border around the top and bottom of the cake. Reserve the remaining vanilla frosting. In a separate bowl, stir ½ cup chocolate frosting and spoon it into a plastic bag. Cut ¼ inch off the tip and pipe a straight border around the top and a wavy border around the bottom of the cake.

Put one taco on the platter along the rounded upper right corner. Lean the other taco against it, wedging a marshmallow under the front side to prop it up. Fix any toppings that may have fallen off.

6 make the refried beans

In a medium bowl, mix 1½ chocolate pudding cups with 1 package Raisinets. Spoon the beans to the left of the tacos and use a small offset spatula to spread them out. Gently press 6 to 8 Raisinets into the beans. Sprinkle the reserved cheese on top.

7 make the rice

Spoon the Rice Krispies cereal below the refried beans. Cut 4 red jujubes and 2 green jujubes in half, and sprinkle them on top of the rice.

8 make the guacamole and sour cream

For the guacamole, in a small bowl, mix the vanilla pudding with equal amounts of green and yellow food coloring to make it lime green; then add 1 teaspoon chocolate frosting to change the color to avocado green. Cut half a green Twizzler into small chunks and mix them into the pudding. Spoon onto the platter. Take the remaining vanilla frosting in the plastic bag and squeeze a swirl next to the guacamole for the sour cream.

steak dinner

When it comes to dinner, give us a thick, well-seasoned grilled steak and we couldn't be happier! This steak is made of pound cake and can be served to either a hungry carnivore or a vegetarian. It would make a fun practical joke at a dinner party, served to the guests with a fork and steak knife, along with a nice glass of wine or beer.

SERVES 2
LEVEL OF DIFFICULTY: 1

special tools

- 1 (10-inch) cardboard cake circle
- Small offset spatula
- #4 round artist's paintbrush
- 1 (11½-inch) dinner plate

ingredients

- 1½ cups vanilla frosting (1 16-ounce can)
- About ⅓ cup mini marshmallows
- 1 (10.75-ounce) frozen pound cake (we use Sara Lee), thawed
- ¾ cup chocolate frosting (from 1 16-ounce can)
- Liquid food coloring: red and black
- 1 teaspoon Nerds, grape flavor
- 1 (3-ounce) package Jelly Belly Peas & Carrots
- 1 yellow Starburst

1 make the mashed potatoes

Refrigerate the vanilla frosting for 15 minutes before you begin. Then, in a medium bowl, stir ½ cup of the frosting until smooth. Add the mini marshmallows and form into a mound in the bowl; refrigerate.

2 make the steak

Using a chef's knife, cut off the top of the pound cake so that it is completely level; the remaining cake should be 1½ inches thick. Lay the cake vertically on a work surface. Referring to the diagram at right, use the tip of the chef's knife to lightly score the outline of the steak into the cake. When you're satisfied that the shape resembles the diagram, cut away the edges and discard them.

Using the blunt edge of the chef's knife, score diagonal grill marks on the cake by pressing the knife in a rocking motion. Rotate the steak and score again, creating a diamond pattern. Position the cake on the cardboard cake circle.

In a small bowl, mix ¼ cup vanilla frosting with 1 tablespoon chocolate frosting and 1 drop red food coloring. Using a small offset spatula, frost the cake with a thin layer on the sides and a very thin layer on top. You want to cover the top of the cake but still see the grill markings. Refrigerate until the frosting is firm, 15 to 20 minutes.

Using the offset spatula, smear a thin layer of chocolate frosting all around the cake, leaving parts of the lighter frosting exposed. In a clean bowl, combine 2 table-spoons vanilla frosting with black food coloring. Smear a thin layer of the black frosting over the chocolate layer, focusing on the edges to give the steak a charred look. Refrigerate until the frosting is firm, 15 to 20 minutes. Reserve the remaining black frosting.

Wet the blunt edge of a chef's knife with cold water and shake off the excess. Starting in the middle of the steak, lightly run the edge along the grill markings to define the indentations. Wet a paper towel with water, wring it out, and then lay it over the top of the steak. Pat gently all over to create a little texture and smooth out the frosting. Refrigerate until the frosting is firm, 15 to 20 minutes.

Using a #4 paintbrush, paint a thin layer of the remaining black frosting in the grooves of the grill markings, using just enough frosting to define the lines but not fill them. Refrigerate the cake.

3 make the black pepper

Put the Nerds in a small bowl. Using the back of a spoon, crush the Nerds to resemble cracked black pepper (covering the bowl with a cloth helps keep the candy from flying out). Add 3 drops of black liquid food coloring and mix with your hand to completely coat the Nerds. Set aside to dry for a few minutes.

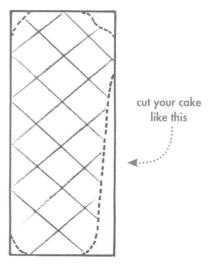

cut your cake like this

4 plate the steak dinner

Using your hand and an offset spatula, carefully place the steak on one side of the dinner plate. Sprinkle the cracked black pepper Nerds over the top. Use a rubber spatula to scoop the mashed potatoes next to the steak, reshaping them into a mound if needed. Push 3 or 4 additional mini marshmallows into the mashed potatoes for texture.

Carefully pour the Jelly Belly Peas & Carrots onto the plate, and put the yellow Starburst in the center. Heat 1 heaping tablespoon of vanilla frosting in a small bowl for 5 to 7 seconds, or until melted, and pour it over the Starburst, letting it run over to create a melting pat of butter.

chinese takeout noodles

This cake looks amazing and is one of the easiest recipes in the book. The portions are just right for two people to share, or you can make one for each guest at a party so everyone has her own box of noodles to enjoy.

chinese takeout

noodles

SERVES 2

LEVEL OF DIFFICULTY: 1

special tools

Small offset spatula

1 (1.5-pint) Chinese takeout container (SEE SOURCES, PAGE 201)

Small piece nonslip shelf liner

ingredients

1 (10.75-ounce) frozen pound cake (we use Sara Lee), thawed

1½ cups vanilla frosting (1 16-ounce can)

2 teaspoons chocolate frosting (from 1 16-ounce can)

Paste or gel paste food coloring: yellow (SEE SOURCES, PAGE 201)

2 Tootsie Roll Midgees

2 Sour Punch Bites, strawberry flavor

1 (3-ounce) package Jelly Belly Peas & Carrots

Chopsticks

1 prepare the takeout box

Lightly trim the top of the pound cake to make it flat, reserving the trimmings. Place the cake horizontally and cut its length in half. Turn the pieces on their sides and cut them in half at a diagonal, resulting in 4 wedge-shaped pieces.

Position 1 cake wedge, wide edge up, in the takeout box. Put a second wedge next to it, wide edge down, then a third wedge, wide edge up. If oriented properly, the wedges will fit together smoothly to fill the box, leaving a small amount of space at the top for noodles. Fill in any gaps using the fourth wedge and the reserved cake trimmings.

2 make the noodles

In a medium bowl, tint 1 cup vanilla frosting with the chocolate frosting and yellow food coloring in small increments to create a noodle color. Refrigerate the frosting until it is quite thick, about 20 minutes.

When the frosting has thickened, spoon it into a zip-top plastic bag and cut ⅛ inch off the tip with scissors. Holding the bag a few inches above the takeout box, squeeze out the noodles continuously, covering the cake first in loose figure-8s and then building more layers in an irregular pattern. Layer the noodles to the top of the box, making sure to reserve a small amount of frosting.

3 add the meat and vegetables

Take the nonslip liner and use it to press down on each of the Tootsie Roll Midgees, slightly flattening the candy and giving it a textured look (see page 12). Arrange the Midgees, the Sour Punch Bites, and 7 peas and 4 carrots in the noodles. With the reserved frosting, add a few noodles over the candy pieces, being careful not to bury them. Add the chopsticks to finish the cake.

sushi platter

This colorful sushi platter is inspired by one of our favorite foods and was the first cake Rick designed for the book. We enjoyed the process of creating this cake and watching each sushi piece come to life. It felt like working on an art project: candies were rolled out and formed, textures were applied, colors were mixed and painted, and the sushi platter itself was the edible canvas.

sushi platter

SERVES 25
LEVEL OF DIFFICULTY: 3

special tools

- 1 (9 × 13-inch) cake board
- Small offset spatula
- Pastry wheel or pizza cutter
- ½-inch flat-head paintbrush
- Small piece of nonslip shelf liner
- 1 round toothpick
- #4 round artist's paintbrush

ingredients

- 1 (8 × 12-inch) sheet cake (¼ sheet) with chocolate frosting
- 1½ cups chocolate frosting (1 16-ounce can)
- 3 Twinkies
- 1½ cups vanilla frosting (1 16-ounce can)
- Cornstarch, for dusting
- Tootsie Fruit Rolls: 6 green, 4 pink, 2 orange, 2 yellow, and 7 vanilla
- 1 cup sweetened coconut flakes, chopped
- 2 orange Swedish Fish
- 1 rope Twizzlers Pull 'n' Peel, cherry flavor
- 1 package Sour Punch Rope, green apple flavor
- 1 tablespoon granulated sugar
- Liquid food coloring: red, yellow, black, and green
- 1 roll Hubba Bubba Bubble Gum Tape, sour green apple flavor
- Pure lemon extract
- 4 Rice Krispies Treats
- 2 Jovy fruit rolls, green apple flavor
- About 18 orange Sixlets
- 1 chocolate Tootsie Roll Midgee
- 1 yellow Starburst
- 1 package Sour Punch Straws, green apple flavor
- ¼ cup vegetable oil
- Chopsticks

1 prepare the cake

Remove the frosting decorations from the cake and trim the cake board (see pages 14 and 15). Put the cake, on its trimmed board, on a 9 × 13-inch cake board and attach with glue.

In a medium bowl, stir the chocolate frosting until smooth. Frost the cake with an offset spatula. Dip the spatula in hot water, shake off the excess, and carefully smooth the frosting. Using a fork, comb the top and sides in a horizontal wave pattern. Clean up the cake board, and refrigerate the cake until the end of Step 2.

2 make the cucumber roll

Cut off and discard the rounded ends of all the Twinkies, and cut each remainder into thirds. Take 4 pieces, hold each with a cream side down, and use an offset spatula to apply a thin layer of vanilla frosting on all sides except the bottom.

Dust the work surface with cornstarch. Smash 3 of the green Tootsie Fruit Rolls into a ball, and use a small rolling pin to roll it into a strip as long and wide as possible. Using a wheel cutter, cut strips the width of the Twinkie pieces. Wrap the iced Twinkie pieces with the strips, cutting off the excess. Dip the iced tops of the Twinkies into the chopped coconut.

Cut 1 orange Swedish Fish into fourths (lengthwise and then in half). Poke a shallow hole into the top of a Twinkie piece and insert a Swedish Fish piece. Cut 2 strands of the Twizzler's Pull 'n' Peel into 8 pieces (about 1½ inches long); insert 2 pieces into the roll. Cut 2 pieces from the Sour Punch Rope (not the Straws), 1½ to

2 inches long, and cut them in half lengthwise. Cut again into halves lengthwise, this time at an angle, so each piece is a triangle. Insert 2 pieces into the Twinkie with the pointed side up. Repeat for the 3 remaining Twinkie pieces.

Remove the cake from the refrigerator and put the cucumber roll pieces on the left side of the platter. Set the cake aside but do not refrigerate.

3 make the sushi roll

Take the 5 remaining Twinkie pieces, hold each piece with a cream side down, and apply a thin layer of vanilla frosting on the sides. On 2 of the pieces, frost the tops as well (these will become the ends of the roll).

Roll the frosted sides in the chopped coconut. Following the process for the cucumber rolls, insert the same cut pieces of Swedish Fish, Sour Punch Rope, and remaining Pull 'n' Peel into the end pieces.

In a small bowl, mix the sugar with 2 drops of red and 2 drops of yellow food coloring to color it orange. Put a small amount on top of each piece as fish roe. Arrange the sushi roll on the platter.

4 make the nigiri sushi

Cut 10 inches of the Bubble Gum Tape and lay it on a sheet of wax paper. In a small bowl, mix ¼ teaspoon black liquid food coloring with ¼ teaspoon lemon extract. Then use a ½-inch flat-head paintbrush to stain the tape black. Cut the tape in half and set both pieces aside to dry.

Cut the length of the Rice Krispies Treats in half. Discard one half. Using your fingers, gently press the remaining 7 halves to form pieces about 2 inches long and 1 inch wide without changing the thickness. (Dust your hands with cornstarch if the pieces get too sticky.) Frost 5 pieces with vanilla frosting on all sides except the bottom, and then roll them in the chopped coconut.

To make the tuna sushi, knead together 2 pink Tootsie Fruit Rolls, adding enough red food coloring to turn the fruit roll red. Press and stretch it until it's about 2½ inches long and no wider than a Rice Krispies rectangle. Score diagonal lines in the top of the "tuna," lightly pressing the edge of an offset spatula halfway through the piece. Spread a little vanilla frosting over the tuna piece to fill the score lines, and scrape off any excess. Put the tuna on top of a prepared Rice Krispies piece and set aside.

To make the salmon sushi, repeat the process used for the tuna, substituting 2 orange Tootsie Fruit Rolls and a mixture of red and yellow food coloring to make a salmon-orange shade. Put the salmon on top of a prepared Rice Krispies piece, and then top it with a small amount of thinly sliced Sour Punch rope for the green onion garnish. Set aside.

To make the egg sushi, shape 2 yellow Tootsie Fruit Rolls into a rectangle about 2¼ inches long. Press a piece of nonslip shelf liner into the top to texture the egg (see page 12), being careful not to change its size. Put the egg on a prepared Rice Krispies Treat, wrap the black gum around the top, and tuck the ends under. Set aside.

To make the shrimp sushi, create a marbled effect by smashing together 1 pink and 2 vanilla

Tootsie Fruit Rolls, being careful not to overmix them. Press this into a teardrop shape, and pinch the end into a tail. Use the spatula to score the shrimp lengthwise down the middle, then 5 across, then several small indentations along the tail. Put the shrimp on a prepared Rice Krispies Treat and set aside.

To make the calamari sushi, repeat the process used for the tuna, substituting 2 vanilla Tootsie Fruit Rolls. Put the calamari on a prepared Rice Krispies Treat, wrap a piece of black gum around it, and tuck the ends under. Set aside.

Arrange all 5 nigiri pieces on the platter below the sushi roll.

5 make the salmon roe and sea urchin sushi

Using the offset spatula, frost 2 of the remaining Rice Krispies Treat pieces with vanilla frosting on all sides except the bottom.

Remove the 2 green fruit rolls from their plastic backing, lightly dust the undersides with cornstarch, and put them back on the plastic. Mix 1 teaspoon each of black liquid food coloring and lemon extract in a small bowl. Using the ½-inch flat-head paintbrush, stain the fruit rolls black; let dry.

Once dry, peel each fruit roll off the plastic and turn it over. Dust the work surface with cornstarch if the fruit roll becomes too sticky. Using a wheel cutter, cut a piece of the fruit roll ¼-inch wider than a Rice Krispies Treat. Wrap each treat with the fruit roll, aligning the bottom of the "seaweed" with the bottom of each Rice Krispies piece and leaving a ¼-inch rim at the top.

To make the salmon roe sushi, put the orange Sixlets on top of a prepared Rice Krispies piece,

adding a small amount of vanilla frosting to make them stick.

To make the sea urchin sushi, smash together 2 vanilla Tootsie Fruit Rolls with half a piece of chocolate Tootsie Roll Midgee. Press this into a shape that fits on top of the remaining prepared Rice Krispies Treat. Using a toothpick, punch small holes over the top. Shape the yellow Starburst into a ball, pressing to flatten it, and put it on the sushi to create an egg yolk. Place the salmon and sea urchin sushi on the cake.

6 make the wasabi and ginger

For the wasabi, smash together 3 green Tootsie Fruit Rolls, half a piece of chocolate Tootsie Roll Midgee, and 1 drop of liquid green food coloring. Form this into an irregular conical shape and put it on the cake. To make the ginger, dust the work surface with cornstarch. Smash together 1 pink Tootsie Roll and 1 vanilla Tootsie Roll, and roll this out to form a thin, irregular circle. Fold it up loosely so that it resembles sliced ginger and put it on the cake.

7 make the platter border

Line the bottom of the cake with the Sour Punch Straws, using scissors to cut them to fit.

8 finish the cake

Use a #4 round paintbrush to brush oil over the sea urchin, tuna, salmon, and calamari sushi. Put the chopsticks, crossed, on the lower right corner of the cake.

ON THE
move

train

This eye-catching train cake is sure to wow your little conductor and put your party on the right track. The shape of train cakes can be a little tricky, so we include a diagram to help you cut and stack the pound cake pieces. Once you have the shape and the cake is frosted, it's just a matter of piping on the accents and placing the cookies and candies to make a spectacular cake.

SERVES 10 TO 15

LEVEL OF DIFFICULTY: 3.5

special tools

Small offset spatula

2 (14-inch) cardboard cake circles

2 (10-inch) cardboard cake circles

13 × 19-inch cake board

2 (½-inch) flat-head paintbrushes

1 (10-inch) wooden skewer

Wire cutters

3 round toothpicks

1-inch flat-head paintbrush

ingredients

3 cups vanilla frosting
(2 16-ounce cans)

Paste or gel paste food coloring:
red, blue, yellow, and black
(SEE SOURCES, PAGE 201)

3 (16-ounce) frozen pound cakes (we use Sara Lee family-size), thawed

1 empty ice cream cone (not a sugar cone)

Small decorating nonpareils, rainbow colored (SEE SOURCES, PAGE 201)

7 black Twizzlers

4 Oreo cookies

2 (1.4-ounce) large York Peppermint Patties

⅓ cup white chocolate melting wafers
(SEE SOURCES, PAGE 201)

1 pack Necco Wafers

1 jumbo marshmallow

1 fudge-striped cookie (we use Keebler)

4 Dots candies: 2 yellow, 1 red, 1 green

1 (2-ounce) package Air Heads Xtremes Sour Belts, lemonade flavor

1 (7-ounce) package sugared candy fruit slices, assorted colors

1 (1.74-ounce) package Peanut M&M's

1 (1.5-ounce) package Giant Chewy SweeTarts

8 Mini Oreo cookies

2 Nerds Ropes, rainbow flavor

1 mini Unicorn Pop

3 Charms Blow Pops

1 Ring Pop

1 (2.17-ounce) package Skittles

1 (1.5-ounce) box jujubes

1 (6-ounce) box Jujyfruits

1 package Starburst

❶ make the engine car

In 4 separate small bowls, mix the following vanilla frosting colors: 1½ cups bright red, ¾ cup a primary blue, ¼ cup plus 2 tablespoons yellow, and ¼ cup plus 2 tablespoons black. Cover the bowls with plastic wrap and set aside.

Lightly trim the tops of the 2 pound cakes flat, and remove the side crusts. Discard the trimmings. Cut even amounts off both ends of the cakes to make each one 8 inches long. Cut one of the loaves in half, making two 4-inch-long pieces. Set the 8-inch loaf (A) horizontally on your work surface and put one of the 4-inch pieces (B) on top of it, flush right.

Position the other 4-inch cake piece on its long side, and cut its thickness in half, making 2 sections (C/D). Lay the cakes out horizontally and score a small "X" onto the tops. Stand each piece on its short end with the "X" facing to the right. To round out the edges where the sides meet the top, measure in ½ inch diagonally from the top and bottom right corners on the top surface, and cut down the full length of both corners to round them off. Discard the corners. Stack piece C, wide side down, horizontally on top of B. Put piece D, wide side down, horizontally on top of A, in front of B.

Scoop ½ cup of the red frosting into a small bowl. Using an offset spatula, attach all the engine car pieces to each other and to a 14-inch cake circle with some of the frosting. Using scissors, trim the excess cardboard flush with the cake. Put the cake, with the cut cardboard, onto a new 14-inch cake circle. Crumb-coat the cake with a thin layer of red frosting. Clean up the cake circle and refrigerate until firm.

❷ make the candy car

Scoop ¼ cup of the blue frosting into a small bowl. Trim the top of the remaining whole pound cake flat, and remove the side crusts.

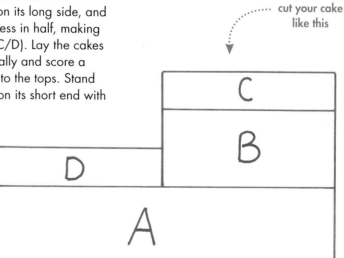

cut your cake like this

Discard the trimmings. Cut even amounts off both ends to make a 6-inch-long cake, and attach it to a 10-inch cake circle, using some of the blue frosting as "glue." Using scissors, trim the excess cardboard flush with the cake. Put the cake, with the cut cardboard, onto a new 10-inch cake circle. Crumb-coat the cake with a thin layer of blue frosting. Clean up the cake circle and refrigerate.

❸ frost the engine and candy cars

Using an offset spatula, frost the engine car with red frosting. Dip the spatula in hot water, shake off the excess, and carefully smooth the frosting. Clean up the board and refrigerate until firm, about 30 minutes. Repeat for the candy car, using blue frosting, and refrigerate until needed.

❹ finish and decorate the engine car

Place the engine car, with the cut cardboard piece still attached, 2 inches from the left edge of a cake board; attach it with frosting.

To create the smokestack, hold the ice cream cone upside down and insert two fingers into the opening. Using two ½-inch flat-head paintbrushes, brush the stem with red frosting, and brush the wide end black. Using a 10-inch skewer, gently punch a hole in the bottom of the cone. Using the skewer as a handle, hold the cone upright, brush more black frosting on the rim, and roll the rim in the rainbow nonpareils. Set the smokestack aside. To start the train track, put 2 black Twizzlers end-to-

end on each side of and flush with the engine car.

To make the wheels, position 2 Oreo cookies and 1 Peppermint Pattie on each side of the engine car. Melt the white chocolate wafers in a microwave-safe bowl at 10-second intervals, stirring until smooth. Spoon the melted chocolate into a zip-top plastic bag and cut ⅛ inch off the tip. Put 1 white Necco Wafer on each wheel, printed side down, and attach with melted chocolate. Cut 1 black Twizzler in half lengthwise and attach the flat side to the Necco wafers with melted chocolate. Hold in place until set.

Spoon the remaining red frosting into a plastic bag and cut ¼ inch off the tip. Pipe 1 small red dot above and below the black Twizzler on each wheel. Pipe a red outline around all edges of the engine car.

Spoon the yellow frosting into a plastic bag and cut ¼ inch off the tip. Pipe the outline of a rectangular window on each side of the engine car, and a half-circle window in front and in back. Fill in with thin horizontal lines. Smooth the frosting windows with an offset spatula dipped in hot water.

Spoon the black frosting into a plastic bag and cut ¼ inch off the tip. Pipe on all black lines and dot details as shown.

Using a wire cutter, trim the 10-inch skewer to 7 inches, preserving the pointed end. Mark the spot for the smokestack on the front of the engine car, and push the flat end of the 7-inch skewer through that spot to the bottom. Put the cone on top and lightly push it into the frosting.

❺ make the puff of smoke

Squeeze the center of the jumbo marshmallow, pinching the top and gently pulling it askew. Put the marshmallow on the exposed skewer tip, covering it completely. If necessary, trim any excess skewer with the wire cutter. Using a ½-inch flat-head paintbrush, apply black frosting to the marshmallow for a smoky effect. Pipe a thin red border around the base of the ice cream cone.

❻ decorate the front of the train

Put the fudge-striped cookie on the front end of the cake with the striped side facing in. With toothpicks, secure the yellow Dots as headlights. Attach the red Dot in the center of the fudge cookie and the green Dot behind the smokestack.

CONTINUES ➡

Cut 2 Sour Belts the width of the train track, and put one flush with the front of the engine car. Cut the other Sour Belt in half lengthwise and put it ½ inch from the other piece. Put the other half piece ½ inch behind the engine car.

Take 2 black sugared fruit slices and adhere them to the front with black frosting, round side down. Pipe black vertical stripes on the slices and outline their edges.

7 connect the engine car and the candy car

Using black frosting, attach 1 green peanut M&M to the back center of the engine car. Keeping the cut cardboard attached for support, attach the blue candy

car behind the engine car with black frosting, touching the green M&M. Extend the track with black Twizzlers and cut off the excess. Attach 1 red Giant Chewy SweeTart to the back center of the candy car and pipe a red dot in the center.

8 decorate the candy car

Put 4 Mini Oreo cookie wheels on each side of the candy car, and pipe a dot of red frosting in the center of each. Line the top edges of the candy car with Nerds Rope, cutting it to fit. Insert the mini Unicorn Pop, Blow Pops, and Ring Pop, and fill the car with M&M's, Skittles, jujubes, Jujyfruits, Necco Wafers, Giant Chewy

SweeTarts, sugared fruit slices, and Starbursts.

Cut 2 Sour Belts the width of the train track, and put one flush with the back of the candy car. Cut the other Sour Belt in half lengthwise and put it ½ inch from the other piece.

9 make the grass

In a bowl, using a 2-to-1 ratio of yellow to blue, mix the remaining yellow and blue frosting together to make green. Using a 1-inch paintbrush and a dabbing motion, apply the frosting to the cake board on both sides of the track. Leave a clean, unfrosted border around the edges of the cake board.

race car

The race car may look intimidating because of its streamlined shape and tricky spoiler piece on the back, but it's worth the effort. While there are car-shaped cake pans on the market, you'll end up with a much cooler cake if you create the car yourself. To avoid the guesswork of making a free-form race car, we use some products that are easy to alter and some that contribute to the shape in their natural state—so this is really about manipulating the cakes. The striking yellow color and sleek design are sure to rev up any race car fanatic's engine.

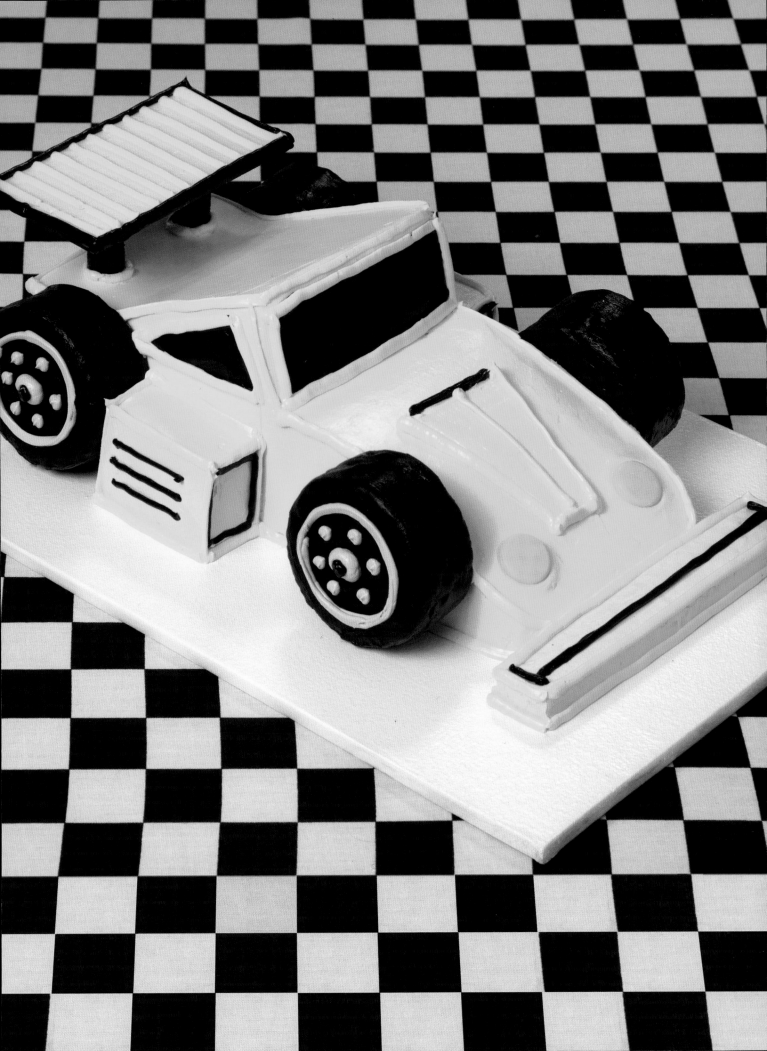

SERVES 7 TO 10

LEVEL OF DIFFICULTY: 3.5

special tools

Small offset spatula

1 (8 × 13-inch) cake board

½-inch flat-head paintbrush

1 (10-inch) cardboard cake circle

3 round toothpicks

ingredients

1 (16-ounce) frozen pound cake (we use Sara Lee family-size), thawed

1 Twinkie

3 cups vanilla frosting (2 16-ounce cans)

Paste or gel paste food coloring: yellow and black (SEE SOURCES, PAGE 201)

4 Ding Dongs

2 vanilla crème wafer cookies (each 2½ inches long)

5 Spree candies: 2 yellow, 2 red, 1 purple

1 Giant Chewy SweeTart, any color

1 Pepperidge Farm Crème Filled Pirouette Rolled Wafer cookie, any flavor

2 tablespoons chocolate melting wafers (SEE SOURCES, PAGE 201)

1 (1.45-ounce) Hershey's dark chocolate bar

1 shape the car

Lightly trim the top of the pound cake to make it flat. Lay the cake horizontally on a work surface. Measure 3 inches in from the right side and score a vertical line across the width. Flip the cake on its side with the scored line facing you; the side is now the top of the cake. Line up a knife from the top of the scored line to the upper right corner of this top surface. Following the scored line with the knife, cut down at this angle, removing a wedge-shaped piece. To make the passenger cabin, lay the cake flat again, put the wedge back in its original position, and then slide the wedge across the cake so it is 1½ inches from the left side.

Cut equal amounts off each end of the Twinkie to make a 3½-inch-long piece, and then cut in half. With the flat, crusted side facing in, put 1 half on each side of the cake, lining them up with the front of the windshield. In a bowl, tint 1½ cups of vanilla frosting yellow. Put ⅓ cup in a separate bowl for crumb-coating; set the remainder aside. Using an offset spatula, attach the cake pieces to each other and to an 8 × 13-inch cake board with a thin layer of frosting. Crumb-coat the entire cake. Clean up the board and refrigerate the cake until firm, 20 to 25 minutes.

2 make the wheels

Using a serrated knife, lightly trim off the jagged bottom edges of the Ding Dongs, leaving the chocolate coating intact. In a bowl, tint ½ cup vanilla frosting black. Using the flat-head paintbrush, apply black frosting to all surfaces of the Ding Dongs. Put them on wax paper on a 10-inch cardboard cake circle, and refrigerate.

3 frost the car

Using the offset spatula, frost the car with the reserved yellow frosting. Dip the spatula in hot water, shake off the excess, and carefully smooth the frosting, being careful to preserve the contours of the car.

4 decorate the car

Put the crème wafer cookies end-to-end at the front of the car and attach them with a little frosting. Then frost the cookies yellow. Spoon the black frosting into a zip-top plastic bag and cut ⅛ inch off the tip. Pipe the outline of the front and side windows, following the car's contours and staying within ¼ inch of the sides. Pipe thin horizontal lines to fill in the windows, and smooth the frosting.

Spoon the remaining yellow frosting into a plastic bag (if you're running low, mix another ¼ cup). Cut ¼ inch off the tip. Outline the windows and all edges of the cake in yellow. On the hood, pipe a triangle that is 2½ inches long, 1½ inches wide at the top, and ½ inch wide at the bottom. Fill in the triangle with thin lines, and then smooth the frosting. Outline the entire triangle except for the top in yellow, and pipe a line down the middle.

Using the black frosting, pipe 3 horizontal lines on the outside wall of each Twinkie half. Then

CONTINUES ➡

pipe a black inner border on the front sides. Pipe a black line across the top of the triangle on the hood and a horizontal capital "I" down the middle of the wafer cookies.

For the headlights, attach 2 yellow Spree candies to the front of the hood, pushing them in gently to create a raised border around them. Attach 2 red Sprees on the back for the taillights, and 1 purple Spree for the exhaust. Refrigerate the car until Step 6.

5 decorate the wheels

In a bowl, tint 2 tablespoons vanilla frosting gray with black food coloring. Spoon it into a zip-top plastic bag and cut ⅛ inch off the tip. To make the wheel detailing, place the Giant Chewy SweeTart in the center of each wheel as a stencil, score a line

around it with a toothpick, and remove the SweeTart. Pipe over the scored lines with the gray frosting. Pipe a larger dot in the center of each circle, and 6 dots around it. Pipe a smaller black dot on the center dot. Refrigerate until needed.

6 make the spoiler

Carefully cut two 1¼-inch-long pieces from each end of the Pirouette wafer. Brush the Pirouette pieces with a small amount of black frosting, leaving the ends exposed. Insert the frosted pieces, cut side down, into the back of the car, spacing them 1 inch apart and ½ inch from the back, making sure they are level. For stability, push a toothpick through each piece so it is flush with the top of the Pirouette. Pipe a yellow border around the base of each.

In a microwave-safe bowl, melt the chocolate wafers at 10-second intervals, stirring until smooth. Spoon into a zip-top plastic bag and cut ⅛ inch off the tip. Break off 1 section of the Hershey's dark chocolate bar and discard it. Frost the bottom of the remaining bar yellow. Attach the frosted chocolate bar to the Pirouette poles using a pea-size amount of melted chocolate. Once the chocolate sets, pipe evenly spaced yellow lines across the bar and a black outline around it.

7 finish the car

For the exhaust, pipe a gray outline around the purple Spree. Use yellow frosting to attach the 2 rear wheels, flush against the Twinkies. Attach the front wheels 1¾ inches from the Twinkies, pushing firmly to get them to stick.

fire engine

Dispatch this fire engine cake at your next party and watch the excitement level reach four alarms! We have streamlined the cake sculpting process by making the fire engine shape with frozen pound cakes. When you are making the wedge cut for the front part of the fire engine, check the step-by-step photos on page 18. It's not as hard as it looks—just read the instructions closely.

SERVES 30 TO 35
LEVEL OF DIFFICULTY: 3.5

special tools

Small offset spatula

1 (9 × 13-inch) cake board

2 (12-inch) cardboard cake circles

1 (10-inch) wooden skewer

8 drinking straws

#4 round artist's paintbrush

9 round toothpicks

ingredients

1 (8 × 12-inch) sheet cake (¼ sheet) with vanilla frosting

6 cups vanilla frosting (4 16-ounce cans)

3 (16-ounce) frozen pound cakes (we use Sara Lee family-size), thawed

Paste or gel paste food coloring: red, black, and blue (SEE SOURCES, PAGE 201)

3 Oreo Cakesters

6 Necco Wafers

1 rope Twizzlers Pull 'n' Peel, cherry flavor

2 yellow Dots

1 small box Jujyfruits

1 large yellow gumdrop

2 red and 1 green Haribo Brixx

1 Haribo Wheel, strawberry flavor

2 (12.4-ounce) packages Twizzlers Rainbow Twists

1 prepare the cake

Remove the frosting decorations from the sheet cake and trim the cake board (see pages 14 and 15). Put the cake, on its trimmed board, on a 9 × 13-inch cake board and attach with glue.

In a medium bowl, stir 1½ cups vanilla frosting until smooth. Using a small offset spatula, frost the sheet cake. Dip the spatula in hot water, shake off the excess, and carefully smooth the frosting. Clean up the board and refrigerate the cake.

2 make the fire engine

Set aside one of the empty pound cake containers. Lightly trim the tops of the pound cakes to make them flat, and remove the side crusts. Put one of the pound cakes on a 12-inch cardboard cake circle and attach it with a thin layer of vanilla frosting. Trim the excess cardboard with scissors, and put the cake, on the trimmed cardboard, onto another 12-inch cardboard cake circle. Set aside.

Put a second pound cake horizontally on your work surface. Using a sharp knife, cut 4 inches off the right side, and discard the remaining piece. Flip the 4-inch piece on its side and cut its thickness in half, discarding one of the halves. Stack the 4-inch piece on top of the third pound cake, flush to one side, and attach it with a thin layer of vanilla frosting.

Put the stacked cake vertically on the work surface with the thick end farthest from you. Use a knife to score a line across the thick end, 1½ inches below the top edge. Flip the cake on its side with the scored line facing to the right. Line up a chef's knife between the top left corner and the beginning of the scored line, and cut down following the line; discard the corner. Flip the cake back over, stack it on top of the pound cake that's on the 12-inch cardboard circle, and attach it with frosting. The cake should now resemble a fire engine.

In a medium bowl, tint 2½ cups plus 2 tablespoons vanilla frosting red, and scoop ¾ cup into a separate bowl for crumb-coating. Set the medium bowl aside. Using an offset spatula, crumb-coat the fire engine with a thin layer of red frosting. Clean up the cardboard and refrigerate the cake until firm, 15 to 20 minutes.

Frost the cake with the reserved red frosting, setting aside ⅓ cup for later use (if there's enough). Carefully smooth the frosting. Clean up the cardboard and refrigerate the cake until firm, 25 to 30 minutes.

3 stack the cakes

Center the empty pound cake container on top of the sheet cake, aligned horizontally, and use a skewer to score a line around the bottom of it. Remove the container.

Make the support to hold up the fire engine by pushing straws vertically into the sheet cake in a 4 × 2 grid pattern, staying within ½ inch of the scored lines. Trim the straws just below the surface of the frosting to hide them. This will allow the fire engine to sit flush with the frosting of the cake. Keeping the trimmed cardboard as a support, put the fire engine on top of the straw structure, centering it over the scored lines. Clean up any damage with a spatula dipped in hot water.

CONTINUES ➡

4 decorate the fire engine

For the wheels, slice through the middle of the frosting of the Oreo Cakesters, scraping off as much frosting as possible. Use the spatula to cover the white cookie frosting with a little red frosting. Attach all 6 wheels to the cake, using the photo as a guide. In a small bowl, tint ⅓ cup vanilla frosting gray with black food coloring. Using a #4 paintbrush, brush gray frosting onto the smooth side and all edges of the Necco Wafers. Attach the unfrosted side of the Neccos to the center of each tire with gray frosting.

In a separate bowl, tint ⅓ cup vanilla frosting black. Spoon the frosting into a zip-top plastic bag and cut ⅛ inch off the tip. Pipe black lines around the edges of the fire truck and across the top of the back, but not around the base of the truck.

Spoon the gray frosting into a plastic bag and cut ⅛ inch off the tip. Pipe the outlines of the 3 windows by following the contours of the cabin and keeping within ½ inch of any black line. Fill them in with thin horizontal lines, and carefully smooth the frosting.

Take ⅓ cup of the remaining red frosting (or make more if necessary), spoon it into a plastic bag, and cut ⅛ inch off the tip.

Pipe a red border around each window, around the base of the fire truck, and over each tire. You may need to pipe a second line over the tires to define the fenders.

Spoon ⅓ cup vanilla frosting into a plastic bag and cut ⅛ inch off the tip. For the ladder, pipe 2 white horizontal lines 1 inch apart, and add about 10 evenly spaced vertical lines between them. Repeat for the ladder on the opposite side. Pipe 7 gray dots around each Necco Wafer wheel and 1 dot in the middle. Pipe 3 dots vertically under the ladders.

For the bumpers, cut two 4-inch pieces of Twizzlers Pull 'n' Peel and lay them across the front and rear of the fire truck. Attach 2 yellow Dots for the headlights with toothpicks. On the front cabin sides, attach 2 round orange Jujyfruits with toothpicks. On top of the cabin, center 1 large yellow gumdrop and 2 red and 1 green Brixx. For each taillight, attach 1 red and 1 yellow oval Jujyfruits with toothpicks 2 inches below the top of the truck.

Pipe a gray border around the top edge of the sheet cake. On top of the truck, pipe 2 gray dots on either side of the red Brixx and 1 gray dot on either side of the green Brixx. Pipe a gray line in the seam above the front and rear bumpers, a large dot on the ends of both bumpers, and a gray line

around the taillights. Above the right taillight, pipe a square with a dot in it. Pull the headlights out, pipe around the circles, and push them back in.

5 make the fire hose

Unravel 5 to 6 inches of the red licorice wheel and put it on the rear of the truck in the upper left corner with the licorice running down clockwise. Bring the hose around to the front and cut the end where it falls flush with the cake. Push a red round Jujyfruit into the center of the licorice wheel with a toothpick to secure it. Attach a black fish-shaped Jujyfruit at the tip of the hose and pipe a gray collar where they meet.

In a small bowl, tint 2 tablespoons vanilla frosting blue. Spoon it into a zip-top plastic bag and cut ¼ inch off the tip. Pipe blue water coming from the hose; then pipe white frosting over the blue.

6 make a border around the cake

Starting from a corner, make a bottom border using the pink Twizzlers, and cut to fit. Stack the orange Twizzlers on the pink, then the yellow Twizzlers on the orange, and cut to fit.

rowboat

The rowboat cake is a great-looking, versatile design that would work equally well for a Father's Day dinner, a retirement party, or a birthday celebration. The peaceful lake setting is even more appealing because of the delicate sugared cattails and the spearmint-scented leaves in the water. With a fish biting at the end of the line, you know it's been a successful day at the lake.

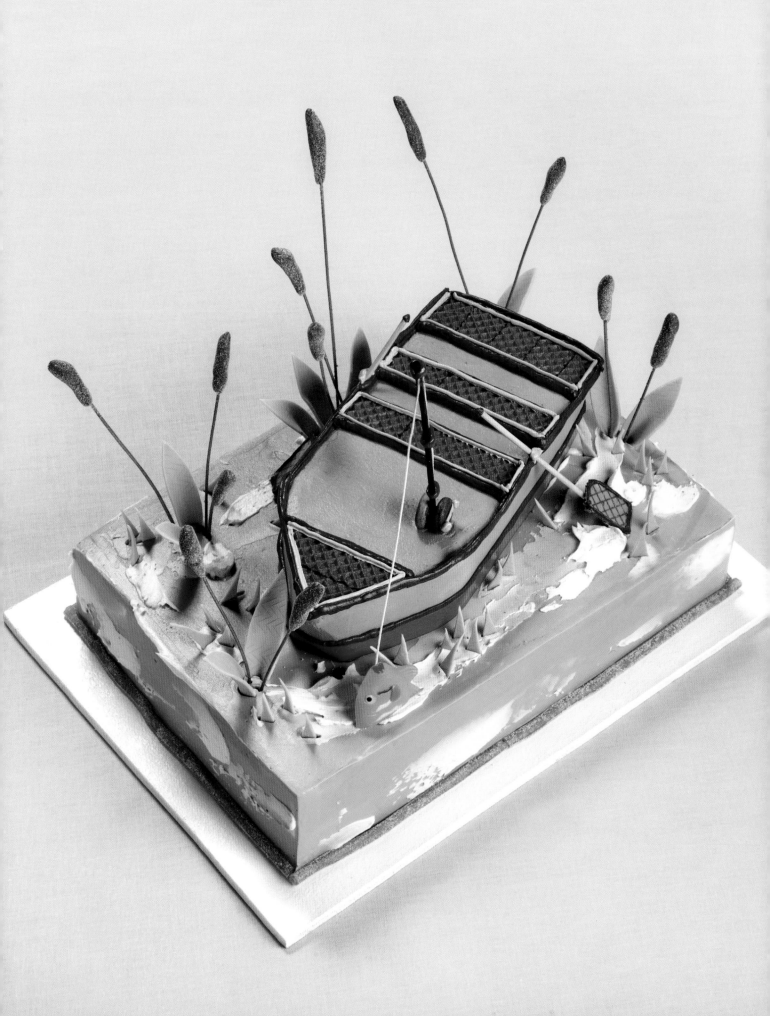

SERVES 25 TO 30
LEVEL OF DIFFICULTY: 2.5

special tools

- Small offset spatula
- 1 (9 × 13-inch) cake board
- 1 (12-inch) cardboard cake circle
- ½-inch flat-head paintbrush
- #4 round artist's paintbrush
- 6 (18- to 20-gauge) green cloth- or paper-covered wires, 18 inches long
- Wire cutters
- 2 (10-inch) wooden skewers
- 1 (22- to 26-gauge) white cloth- or paper-covered wire, 18 inches long

ingredients

- 1 (8 × 12-inch) sheet cake (¼ sheet) with vanilla frosting
- 3 cups vanilla frosting (2 16-ounce cans)
- Paste or gel paste food coloring: blue and yellow (SEE SOURCES, PAGE 201)
- 1 (16-ounce) frozen pound cake (we use Sara Lee family-size), thawed
- ¾ cup chocolate frosting (from 1 16-ounce can)
- 1 roll Hubba Bubba Bubble Tape, Awesome Original flavor
- Liquid food coloring: red and black
- Pure lemon extract
- 5 chocolate wafer cookies (each about 2½ inches long)
- 4 Tootsie Roll Midgees
- ½ cup granulated sugar
- 2 purple Spree candies
- 1 gummy fish of choice
- 7 Sour Punch Straws, green apple flavor
- 10 sticks Wrigley's Spearmint gum

❶ prepare the cake

Remove the frosting decorations from the sheet cake and trim the cake board (see pages 14 and 15). Put the cake, on its trimmed board, on a 9 × 13-inch cake board and attach with glue.

In a bowl, tint 1½ cups vanilla frosting blue. Using an offset spatula, frost the sheet cake. Dip the spatula in hot water, shake off the excess, and carefully smooth the frosting. Clean up the board and refrigerate the cake.

❷ make the rowboat

Lightly trim the top of the pound cake to make it flat. Put the cake horizontally on a work surface. Measure 3 inches from the left side, and use a knife to score a line there across the width. Find the center point of the left edge, and score two lines from that point to each end of the scored line, forming a triangle. Cut off and discard the corners.

Flip the cake over. Measure 1 inch from the pointed end. Position your knife across the width of the cake at that spot, then angle the knife toward the base of the point and slice down at a diagonal. Discard the cut piece. When you flip the cake back over, it should resemble a rowboat.

Put the cake on a 12-inch cardboard cake circle. In a bowl, mix ¾ cup vanilla frosting, 1 tablespoon chocolate frosting, and enough yellow food coloring to make a tan color. Scoop 2 tablespoons of the tan frosting into a separate bowl for crumb-coating; set the remainder aside. Using an offset spatula, crumb-coat the cake. Refrigerate until firm, about 20 minutes.

Using the reserved tan frosting, frost the entire cake. Carefully smooth the frosting. Clean up the cardboard and refrigerate the cake until firm, 20 to 25 minutes.

❸ decorate the rowboat

Put a 25-inch-long piece of wax paper on the work surface and unroll a 24-inch-long strip of the bubblegum tape. In a small bowl, mix ¼ teaspoon liquid red food coloring with ½ teaspoon lemon extract. Using a ½-inch flat-head paintbrush, brush one side of the bubblegum tape red; let dry for a few minutes. Position the rowboat on the work surface with the pointed end facing left. Starting on the back side, wrap the bubblegum tape around the base of the rowboat, and cut it to fit. Clean the flat-head paintbrush and use it to help contour the tape around the front tip of the rowboat.

Split open the chocolate wafer cookies using the edge of an offset spatula. Use the spatula to separate the filling from the cookie, and discard it. Starting at the front of the boat, put 2 wafers side-by-side, and cut away the excess with scissors to fit the shape of the boat. Cut 3 wafers in half, and at the back of the boat, line up 5 of the pieces with the ends flush with the back edge. Cut to fit.

Starting 1 inch from the back row of wafers, lay down 2 wafers end-to-end and cut to fit. Repeat with 2 more wafers 1 inch in front of the previous row. Set aside the 1 remaining wafer. Refrigerate the cake until firm, 20 to 25 minutes.

Once the rowboat and the sheet cake are firm, carefully lift the boat off the cardboard and put it on the sheet cake at a diagonal, slightly off-center, leaving more space in front of the boat.

In a small bowl, stir ¼ cup chocolate frosting until smooth, then spoon it into a zip-top plastic bag and cut ⅛ inch off the tip. Pipe a line at the seam of the red bubble tape and the tan frosting around the boat. Pipe a border around the top edge of the rowboat and a border around the wafer sections to define the seating. In a small bowl, tint 2 tablespoons vanilla frosting gray with black food coloring. Spoon it into a plastic bag and cut ⅛ inch off the tip. Pipe a gray border around all the wafer sections.

④ make the lake scene

In a small bowl, stir ¼ cup vanilla frosting until smooth. Using an offset spatula, lightly smear the frosting with uneven strokes over the blue frosting to add texture. Smear a small amount around the boat to make waves. Refrigerate the cake only as long as it takes to complete the next step. Refrigeration overnight before completing the cake is not recommended, as the colors could bleed.

For the cattails, cut 3 of the Tootsie Roll Midgees into quarters. Cut 6 cloth- or paper-covered green wires in half with a wire cutter. Form the 12 Tootsie Roll pieces into oval cattails, varying

in size from 1 to 1¼ inches, and insert the end of a cut green wire into each. Put the sugar in a small bowl and roll the cattails in the sugar.

Insert the cattails into the cake in 5 groupings, with their heights ranging from 3½ to 8 inches (cut the wires as needed).

⑤ make the oars and fishing pole

Cut 1 wooden skewer in half and insert it into the lake cake at an angle so that it is leaning against the middle of the boat, with 2½ inches exposed above the boat. Cut the remaining wafer cookie in half and lightly smear some of the tan frosting over the top of each half. Put a wafer half at the base of the skewer where it meets the water, and attach it with a dot of chocolate frosting. Pipe a border around the oar paddle and a dot at the tip of the handle. Where the oar joins the rowboat, pipe a gray line over the oar. Repeat the process on the opposite side with the second oar.

In a small bowl, mix ½ tea-spoon black liquid food coloring with ¼ teaspoon lemon extract. Using a #4 paintbrush, paint the remaining wooden skewer black and let dry. Bend a white cloth- or paper-covered wire in half, and hold it against the skewer with the bend at the top. Loop the wire

once around the skewer to secure it, and loop the end of the wire around the base of the skewer to attach it at the bottom.

Insert the skewer through the rowboat, to the bottom of the lake cake. Insert the end of the loose half of the wire into the water at the front of the boat. Attach 1 purple Spree to each side of the base of the fishing pole with a piped dot of gray frosting. Pipe 1 line across and 2 dots on both ends of each Spree to make the pole handle. Take the remaining Tootsie Roll, break off 3 small pieces, and roll them into 3 tubes. Wrap 1 tube around the top of the fishing pole, and the other tubes 2 inches apart on the pole, joining the wire and the pole. Cut the head from a gummy fish and put it in the water, lining up the fish's mouth with the fishing line.

⑥ make a border around the cake

Starting at a back corner, make a border around the bottom of the sheet cake with green Sour Punch Straws, cutting them to fit.

⑦ make the leaves of the cattails

Using scissors, cut the sticks of gum into wide leaf shapes, reserving the trimmings. To form the leaves, cup each one at the middle to curl it up and pinch the bottom of the leaf. The curl is important for structural support. Insert the leaves into the cake in groups around the cattails. Scatter the trimmings in the lake, around the boat and cattails.

B-2
stealth bomber

The B-2 Spirit Stealth Bomber is one of the most powerful aircrafts in the U.S. Air Force. Its unique shape makes for a striking cake that would be perfect for someone in the military or for anyone who has a fascination with the B-2 or with planes in general. It won't take an aircraft engineer to make this cake. Just follow the measurements and marks in the recipe and cut the sheet cake to form the distinct triangular shape. Frost it a dark gray, then watch your cake take flight.

SERVES 25

LEVEL OF DIFFICULTY: 2.5

special tools

1 (8-inch) cardboard cake circle

1 (14 × 21-inch) cake board

Small offset spatula

ingredients

1 (12 × 16-inch) sheet cake (½ sheet) with vanilla frosting

1 (10.75-ounce) frozen pound cake (we use Sara Lee), thawed

2 Twinkies

4½ cups vanilla frosting (3 16-ounce cans)

Paste or gel paste food coloring: black and blue (SEE SOURCES, PAGE 201)

1 prepare the cake

Remove the frosting decorations from the sheet cake (see page 14). When removing the frosting, be careful to keep the cake's rectangular shape because precise measurements are needed.

2 mark the shape of the B-2

Put the sheet cake horizontally on a work surface. You'll start by measuring and marking the shape of the cake, and then you'll make cuts. First, measure the top (long) edge of the cake with a ruler, find the center, and mark that spot with a knife.

Make the second mark on the left edge by measuring 8 inches straight down from the top left corner.

Make the third mark 3 inches over and 8½ inches down from the top left corner.

Make the fourth mark on the bottom edge of the cake, 5½ inches from the bottom left corner.

Make the fifth mark 6½ inches over and 10½ inches down from the top left corner.

Measure the bottom edge of the cake with a ruler, find the center, and make the sixth mark.

Make the seventh mark 6½ inches over and 10½ inches down from the top right corner.

Make the eighth mark on the bottom edge of the cake, 5½ inches from the bottom right corner.

Make the ninth mark 3 inches over and 8½ inches down from the top right corner.

Make the final mark on the right edge of the cake by measuring 8 inches straight down from the top right corner. The marks should all be a mirror image of each other from the center of the cake.

3 cut out the B-2

note: discard all trimmings unless otherwise noted

Using a chef's knife, cut a straight line between mark 1 and mark 2.

Cut a straight line between the bottom left corner and mark 3. Cut a straight line between mark 3 and mark 4, reserving the trimming.

Cut a straight line between mark 4 and mark 5. Cut a straight line between mark 5 and mark 6.

Cut a straight line between mark 6 and mark 7. Cut a straight line between mark 7 and mark 8.

Cut a straight line between mark 8 and mark 9. Cut a straight line between mark 9 and the bottom right corner.

Cut a straight line between mark 10 and mark 1.

Put the 1 piece of reserved trimming (from the bottom left corner) in its original orientation before you cut it. Cut the piece in half to make 2 triangles. Position 1 triangle at the tip of each wing at the bottom left and right edges of the cake and attach them with a little frosting. The triangles should form right angles.

Take the pound cake and cut its thickness in half. Discard the bottom piece. Lay the pound cake down vertically on your work surface, measure 1 inch from the top edge, and score a line across. Reorient the pound cake horizontally with the scored line to the right. Flip the cake on its side with the scored line facing you. Line up a knife on the top surface between the beginning of the scored line and the top right corner on the same surface. Cut down following the scored line, and discard the trimming. Restore the cake to its original position, put it onto an 8-inch cardboard cake circle, and set aside.

Putting the Twinkies flat side down, cut equal amounts off both ends to make two 3-inch-long pieces. Cut the thickness of each Twinkie in half, discard the flat half, and put the 2 domed pieces on separate plates; set aside.

4 frost the B-2

Trim all excess cake board by pulling the B-2 cake just over the counter's edge. Because of the angled cuts on the cake, a combination of a knife and scissors is best to cut flush around the perimeter. Center the cake, with the trimmed board, on a new cake board, and glue it down.

In a bowl, tint 3 cups of vanilla frosting charcoal gray with black food coloring. Separate 1 cup of the frosting, and crumb-coat all the cake pieces with gray frosting. (Start with the Twinkies and the pound cake, and then do the B-2 bomber cake.) Clean up the cake circle, plates, and cake board, and refrigerate until firm, 15 to 20 minutes.

Using the remaining charcoal gray frosting, and working with the pieces one at a time from the refrigerator, frost the Twinkies and then the pound cake. Smooth the frosting and refrigerate. Next, frost the B-2 bomber. Smooth the frosting and refrigerate until firm, about 30 minutes.

5 assemble the B-2

Put the pound cake vertically on top of the B-2 with the angled side flush with the top edge and centered. Align the Twinkies pieces vertically on either side of the pound cake, spaced ½ inch from it and centered on the bomber.

6 pipe on the details

In a small bowl, tint ¼ cup vanilla frosting black with food coloring. Spoon it into a zip-top plastic bag and cut ⅛ inch off the tip. Orient the cake with the front of the B-2 bomber facing you, and pipe a black outline around the slanted portion of the pound cake (the cockpit area). Fill in the outline with thin horizontal lines, and carefully smooth the frosting.

Pipe a black border around the front-facing sides of the Twinkies (the engine intake areas) and fill them in with thin horizontal lines. On the back-facing side of the Twinkies (the engine exhaust), pipe a black border and fill it in as above. Carefully smooth the frosting.

In a small bowl, tint ⅓ cup vanilla frosting charcoal gray, mixing in any leftover (non-crumb-coat) gray frosting. Spoon it into a plastic bag and cut ¼ inch off the tip. Pipe a top edge border around the entire plane.

On the top center of the pound cake, pipe a vertical line from the slanted area to the back edge. Pipe a gray border around the cockpit window, and one around the back-facing side of the pound cake to frame it. Pipe a border around the base of the pound cake on the left and right sides.

Starting at the top of the cockpit window, ½ inch from the centerline, pipe a 3-inch-long vertical line on both sides. Pipe a longer line on each side spanning the length of the pound cake along both top edges. On each Twinkie, pipe 3 horizontal lines ¼ inch apart, starting in the center and moving forward. Outline the front- and back-facing sides of the Twinkies around the top arc, not around the base.

Using the black frosting, pipe an inner border that outlines the B-2 bomber and is ¼ inch from the gray outer border.

Stir 2 tablespoons vanilla frosting until smooth, spoon it into a plastic bag, and cut ⅛ inch off the tip. Use the photo as a guide to pipe the white line accents (next to the charcoal gray lines, not on top of them): around the tip of the B-2, around the cockpit windows, and next to the 3 horizontal lines on the Twinkies. Also pipe accents around the wing tips and the back side.

7 make the sky

In a small bowl, tint ½ cup vanilla frosting sky blue. Spread a thin layer of blue frosting all around the B-2 on the cake board. Use a damp towel and the spatula to remove a border of the frosting from the board, leaving an unfrosted edge.

In a small bowl, stir 2 tablespoons vanilla frosting until smooth, and smear irregular strokes over the sky to make clouds. Spoon the remaining blue frosting into a zip-top plastic bag, cut ¼ inch off the tip, and pipe a border to frame the whole rectangle.

8 make the border

Finish the cake with a piped charcoal gray bottom border around the B-2 where the cake meets the board.

GOING
retro

banana split

There is nothing like an old-fashioned banana split—until it starts melting faster than you can eat it! We've fixed that problem by making a cake that looks just like this beloved ice cream parlor treat. It's a cinch to make with a difficulty level of 1, and you won't believe how real it looks.

SERVES 2 TO 4

LEVEL OF DIFFICULTY: 1

special tools

1 glass or plastic banana split dish

Small offset spatula

ingredients

3 Hostess CupCakes, any flavor

3 Ding Dongs

2 Oreo Cakesters

1½ cups vanilla frosting
(1 16-ounce can)

3 round vanilla wafer cookies

Paste or gel paste food coloring:
pink, red, and yellow (SEE SOURCES,
PAGE 201)

¾ cup chocolate frosting (from
1 16-ounce can)

2 Twinkies

1 (8.4-ounce) can Betty Crocker
Cupcake Icing, Cloud White

1 tablespoon chopped unsalted
peanuts

1 teaspoon decorating nonpareils,
assorted colors

3 red gumballs

1 make the base

Take the Hostess CupCakes and cut
¼ inch off 2 sides of each cupcake.
Line them up on the bottom of a
banana split dish with the flat sides
together, and set aside.

2 make the ice cream scoops

Take the Ding Dongs, and using a
paring knife, cut off ¼ inch of the
top edge of each one. Separate
2 Oreo Cakesters and put 3 halves,
frosting side down, on top of the
Ding Dongs (discard the extra
half). Using a little vanilla frosting,
attach 1 vanilla wafer, flat side
down, to the top of each Cakester.
Put each of the 3 scoops on a
separate plate.

In a small bowl, stir ¼ cup
vanilla frosting until smooth.
Using a small offset spatula,
crumb-coat each scoop with a
thin layer of frosting, filling in the
gaps to create a rounded shape.
Refrigerate until the frosting is firm,
about 15 minutes. Meanwhile,
prepare three frostings: In the first
bowl, stir ¼ cup vanilla frosting
until smooth. In the second bowl,
tint ¼ cup vanilla frosting light
pink. In the third bowl, mix ¼ cup
vanilla frosting with 2 tablespoons
chocolate frosting.

Frost each ice cream scoop
a different color, for chocolate,
vanilla, and strawberry flavors.
When they're slightly firm, run the
back of the offset spatula from
the base of each scoop up to and
over the top, all the way around,
to round it off. Dip the spatula in
hot water, shake off the excess,
and carefully smooth the frosting.
Refrigerate the scoops until firm,
about 30 minutes. Then arrange
the scoops in the banana split dish
with the chocolate scoop in the
middle.

3 make the bananas

Cut 1 Twinkie in half lengthwise
and put the cream-filled side
against the ice cream scoops,
flat side down. Slightly angle the
Twinkie halves, pressing them to
the shape of the bowl. Repeat
with a second Twinkie on the
other side. Refrigerate while you
prepare the toppings.

4 make the toppings

Use 3 small microwave-safe
bowls for the toppings. For
the strawberry topping, tint
2 tablespoons vanilla frosting a
dark pink, and melt it for 4 to
7 seconds in the microwave. Stir
with an offset spatula, and set
aside. For the chocolate topping,
melt 2 tablespoons chocolate
frosting for 4 to 7 seconds in the
microwave, stir, and set aside.
For the butterscotch frosting, mix
5 teaspoons vanilla frosting with
1 teaspoon chocolate frosting and
enough yellow food coloring to
make a butterscotch color. Melt for
7 to 10 seconds in the microwave,
stir, and set aside.

Starting with the strawberry
scoop, slowly pour the strawberry
topping over it, making sure it
drizzles down the ice cream
but doesn't completely cover it.
Repeat with the chocolate and
butterscotch toppings on the
chocolate and vanilla scoops,
respectively.

5 make the whipped cream

Use the star tip on the Betty
Crocker Cupcake Icing to make
the whipped cream. (Practice
making the whipped cream
swirl on a separate plate before
topping the ice cream.) Make a
swirl on each ice cream scoop,
starting with an outer ring and
gradually spiraling upward.

6 finish the cake

Sprinkle the chopped peanuts and
nonpareils over the ice cream, and
then top each scoop with 1 red
gumball for a cherry.

roller skate

Go back in time to the late '70s and early '80s, and lace up those roller skates at the local skating rink! Many fun memories inspired this roller skate cake, with its pink wheels and toe stop and a rainbow pattern on the boot. With its high-impact upright design, it'll take a little longer to complete, but the time invested will be well worth the ecstatic reaction you get when your guests see it.

SERVES 20 TO 25

LEVEL OF DIFFICULTY: 4

special tools

Small offset spatula

4 (10-inch) cardboard cake circles

2 (12-inch) cardboard cake circles

1 (12 × 20-inch) thick, sturdy cake board

8 drinking straws

3 (10-inch) wooden skewers

½-inch flat-head paintbrush

ingredients

7½ cups vanilla frosting (5 16-ounce cans)

Paste or gel paste food coloring: pink and black (SEE SOURCES, PAGE 201)

8 Ding Dongs

4 (16-ounce) frozen pound cakes (we use Sara Lee family-size), thawed

1 roll peppermint Life Savers

1 (12.4-ounce) package Twizzlers Rainbow Twists

4 Necco Wafers, any color

28 pink Necco Candy Buttons

1 jumbo marshmallow

① make the wheels

In separate mixing bowls, tint 1½ cups vanilla frosting pink, and tint ¾ cup vanilla frosting black. Cover the black frosting with plastic wrap and set aside.

Attach the bottoms of 2 Ding Dongs with pink frosting to make 1 wheel; repeat for the other 3 wheels. Position each wheel on a separate plate, and frost them pink using an offset spatula; refrigerate until firm, about 20 minutes. Frost each wheel two more times, until there is no brown peeking through, refrigerating about 15 minutes between layers. On the final frosting, dip an offset spatula in hot water, shake off the excess, and smooth the wheels. Refrigerate until needed.

② make the base of the skate

Take 2 of the pound cakes, lightly trim the tops to make them flat, and remove the side crusts, reserving the trimmings. Cut equal amounts off the left and right ends of the cakes to make two 8-inch-long loaves.

Take the first trimmed pound cake, lay it down vertically on a work surface, and flip it on its side. Cut a ½-inch slice off the right side to reduce its thickness. Stack the cut ½-inch section on top of the second pound cake to make the base. Use a small amount of black frosting to "glue" the layers together. Set aside the rest of the first pound cake (it will become piece B in the boot).

Trim equal amounts off each long side of the stacked pound cake (the base) to make a 3-inch-wide loaf. The new loaf should

now measure 8 inches by 3 inches and will form the support for the roller skate.

Attach the base to a 10-inch cardboard cake circle using black frosting. Trim off all excess cardboard with scissors or a knife. To add height to the base, attach two more 10-inch cardboard cake circles underneath, gluing the base and trimming the excess cardboard as before. Put the cake and cardboard on a fourth 10-inch cardboard circle but do not attach with glue. Frost the base and the cardboard layers with black frosting, and refrigerate.

③ shape the boot

Take the remaining 2 pound cakes, and lightly trim the tops and the sides, reserving the trimmings. One of these pound cakes will become piece A in the diagram. Set aside the second pound cake (it will become pieces C and D).

Take the cake slice that was set aside in Step 2 (piece B) and position it horizontally on a work surface. The cake should be 8 inches long. Flip it on its long side and make a mark with a chef's knife on the top edge, 5 inches from the left. Line up the knife at an angle between the mark and the bottom right corner on the same surface, and cut through, discarding the cut piece. Put the trimmed piece flush left on top of piece A with the wedge cut facing right.

For the top of the boot, take the pound cake set aside for pieces C and D, and cut equal amounts off both ends to make the cake 9 inches long. Cut it into 2 pieces, one 5 inches long (piece C) and the second 4 inches long (piece

CONTINUES ➡

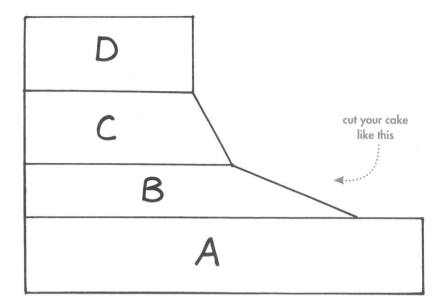

cut your cake
like this

D). Flip piece C on its long side and make a mark on the top edge, 4 inches from the left. Line up the knife at an angle between the mark and the bottom right corner on the same surface and cut through, discarding the cut piece. Put piece C flush left on top of piece B with the wedge cut facing right.

Finish assembling the boot by putting piece D on top of piece C. Refer to the diagram to make sure the boot looks correct before proceeding. Use the chef's knife to make any necessary trims. Disassemble the boot pieces.

4 assemble and frost the boot

In a medium bowl, stir 1½ cups vanilla frosting until smooth for the crumb coat. Attach the bottom piece of the boot to a 12-inch cardboard cake circle with frosting. Trim off all excess cardboard. Put the cake, with the cardboard, on a new 12-inch cardboard cake circle.

Reassemble the boot, attaching each piece with a thin layer of vanilla frosting. Fill in any gaps with the reserved cake trimmings. Crumb-coat the boot with a thin layer of vanilla frosting. Clean up the cake circle and refrigerate until firm, about 20 minutes.

In a medium bowl, stir 3 cups vanilla frosting until smooth, and frost the boot. Dip the spatula in hot water, shake off the excess, and carefully smooth the frosting. Clean up the cake circle and refrigerate the cake until firm.

5 attach the boot to the base

Take the black frosted cake and glue the bottom cardboard to the middle of a sturdy cake board. A structural upright cake needs a strong board—like a sheet pan, wrapped cake board, or platter— to support its weight. Make the support for the boot by pushing the straws vertically into the black cake, evenly spaced, cutting each straw just below the surface of the frosting.

Put the boot cake, with its cardboard bottom, on top of the black base with the back end of the boot hanging over the base by about ¼ inch. Push 1 skewer into the center of the boot opening, and 2 skewers 3½ inches from the tip of the boot. Using a hammer, push the skewers through to the bottom of the cake. Use wire cutters to cut off any excess just below the frosting line. Repair any damage by smoothing over with vanilla frosting.

6 decorate the skate

Spoon the remaining vanilla frosting into a zip-top plastic bag and cut ¼ inch off the tip. Pipe a border all around the boot. To make the holes for the laces, starting ½ inch from the top, put 5 evenly spaced peppermint Life Savers on each side. Start the laces with the bottom row, connecting the 2 holes with a piped line. To create thick laces, pipe over each line two to three times. Make "X"s through the remaining 4 holes, piping over the lines multiple times before crisscrossing.

To make the rainbow, put one end of a blue Twizzler against the left side of the boot and curve it to the bottom, using the entire length of the Twizzler. Follow the same curved line with the rest of the Twizzler colors, cutting any excess. Repeat on the other side of the boot.

Starting from the top Life Saver, on each side of the shoe, pipe a loose "S"-curved shoelace over the rainbow, matching its thickness to the rest of the laces.

7 attach the wheels

Work with 1 wheel at a time, keeping the others firm in the

refrigerator until needed. With the brown side of the wheel facing the black base, put the back wheels ¼ inch from the back edge and the front wheels ¾ inch from the front. If the wheels are damaged during placement, repair them with pink frosting.

With your finger, smudge black frosting on the unprinted side of the Necco Wafers and put 1 in the center of each wheel, with the frosted side facing out. Put 7 pink Necco Candy Buttons on each wheel, evenly spaced. Squeeze the excess vanilla frosting into a new zip-top plastic bag and cut ⅛ inch off the tip. Pipe a line from the center of each pink candy to the center of the Necco wafer.

In a bowl, mix the remaining vanilla frosting with black frosting to tint it a medium gray, spoon it into a plastic bag, and cut ⅛ inch off the tip. Pipe 1 dot in the center of each Necco Wafer where the lines meet. Pipe a half-moon around the center of each Life Saver where the laces touch and a thin line across the "S" laces, about ½ inch from the bottom. Cut an additional ⅛ inch off the tip of the gray frosting bag and pipe a border around the top opening of the boot.

8 make the suspension from the boot to the wheels

Starting at the center edge of one wheel, pipe a thick line (by piping two or three times over itself) from the wheel to the base of the boot.

Repeat for the right and left gray lines, angling them slightly. Repeat on the 3 other wheels.

9 make the toe stop

Using a ½-inch paintbrush, apply a thin layer of pink frosting to all sides of the marshmallow except for one end. Use vanilla frosting to attach the white end to the boot at a slight angle, and press it into place.

retro radio

Before the television was introduced, radios brought families together to listen to music, news, and other special programming. They came in all sorts of decorative designs, sometimes small and sometimes quite large. Most people don't own radios today, save the ones that are in their car, but retro radios are making a comeback because people love them as beautiful art pieces. This one looks so cool, you won't want to eat it.

SERVES 15
LEVEL OF DIFFICULTY: 3

special tools

- 3 (14-inch) cardboard cake circles
- Small offset spatula
- Large offset spatula
- ½-inch flat-head paintbrush
- 1 (9 × 12-inch) cake board, 2-ply-thick
- 3 round toothpicks
- 2 (18-gauge) white cloth- or paper-covered wires, 18 inches long
- Wire cutters

ingredients

- 3 (16-ounce) frozen pound cakes (we use Sara Lee family-size), thawed
- 4½ cups vanilla frosting (3 16-ounce cans)
- Paste or gel paste food coloring: black and red (SEE SOURCES, PAGE 201)
- 6 Giant Chewy SweeTarts: 5 purple and 1 red (from 5 1.5-ounce packages)
- ½ cup chocolate melting wafers (SEE SOURCES, PAGE 201)
- 1 (4.5-ounce) package Sour Punch Straws, strawberry flavor
- 1 rope Twizzlers Pull 'n' Peel, cherry flavor
- 1 large red gumdrop
- 3 Life Savers, cherry flavor
- 2 red Dots
- 7 jujubes: 6 purple and 1 red
- 2 red oval Jujyfruits
- 1 red gumball, machine refill size

① prepare the cake

Trim the tops of the pound cakes to make them flat, and remove the side crusts, making each loaf 3½ inches by 9 inches. Reserve the trimmings. In a bowl, tint 3 cups vanilla frosting black. Scoop 1 cup black frosting into a separate bowl for crumb-coating.

Attach one of the pound cakes to a 14-inch cardboard cake circle, using black frosting as "glue." Put the 2 other cakes on top of the first cake, bottoms facing up. Using a small offset spatula and the bowl of crumb-coat frosting, spread a thin layer of frosting between the layers. Fill any gaps in the corners with the reserved cake trimmings.

Trim the excess on the cardboard cake circle by pulling the cake just over the counter's edge. Using a chef's knife or serrated bread knife, cut flush around the cake with a sawing motion. Put the cake, with the trimmed cardboard still attached, onto a new 14-inch cardboard cake circle. Use a large offset spatula to crumb-coat the cake with the black frosting. Refrigerate the cake until the frosting is firm, about 20 minutes. Then frost the cake black again. Dip the spatula in hot water, shake off the excess, and carefully smooth the frosting. Clean up the cake circle and refrigerate the cake.

② make the radio's feet

Using the ½-inch flat-head paintbrush, brush black frosting around the edges of 1 purple Giant SweeTart, being careful not to touch the top or bottom. Repeat with 4 more purple SweeTarts, and

set them aside. Melt the chocolate wafers in a microwave-safe bowl at 10-second intervals, stirring until smooth. Spoon the chocolate into a zip-top plastic bag and cut ⅛ inch off the tip.

Cut a 12 × 5-inch piece of wax paper and put it on top of the cake. Put the third 14-inch cardboard cake circle on top of the wax paper. With one hand on top of the cake and the other supporting the bottom, quickly turn the cake upside down. Remove the 14-inch cardboard cake circle that's now on top by running a large offset spatula between it and the trimmed cake circle. Do not remove the attached trimmed cardboard.

Pipe a pea-size amount of melted chocolate onto the 5 prepared SweeTarts. Attach them to the four corners of the trimmed cardboard and attach one to the middle of the cardboard. Pipe another pea-size dollop of chocolate on the SweeTarts. Attach the 2-ply-thick cake board, centered as best as you can, pressing gently to attach.

Flip the cake over and pull off the 14-inch cake circle, leaving the wax paper attached. Refrigerate the cake until the frosting is firm, about 30 minutes. Then remove the cake from the refrigerator and gently pull off the wax paper. If necessary, fix any damage with frosting and/or an offset spatula dipped in hot water.

③ make the tuning dial and speaker

Take a clean frosting lid (that isn't warped) and put the inner side of the lid against the cake, ½ inch from the top and right edges.

Lightly score the area by pressing the lid gently into the cake; remove the lid. Spoon ½ cup vanilla frosting into a zip-top plastic bag and cut ¼ inch off the tip. Pipe a line over the scored circle, and fill it in by piping thin rings, working inward. Smooth the frosting carefully using a small offset spatula dipped in hot water.

To make the speaker, start at the left side, ½ inch from the top and from the side. Using the vanilla frosting, pipe a line 4 inches across and another line 4½ inches down on the left side. Continue piping the bottom and right side to outline the speaker, which should be 4 inches wide by 4½ inches high. Fill in by piping thin white lines until the area is covered, and smooth it over.

Cut 10 red Sour Punch Straws into 4-inch-long pieces, or to fit the width of the speaker. Starting at the top edge, put 10 straw pieces horizontally and evenly spaced over the speaker. Scoop ½ cup black frosting into a plastic bag, and cut ¼ inch off the tip. Pipe a border around the speaker box and the tuning dial, covering the seam where the white frosting meets the black.

Starting at the bottom of the tuning dial, outline the inside of the black piped line with 1 strand of the Twizzlers Pull 'n' Peel, and cut it to fit. If the licorice isn't long enough, fill in with a small piece of another strand. Cut another strand of the licorice into four 2½-inch-long pieces. Put 1 piece around the top of each foot and tuck the ends under the radio.

In a small bowl, tint 1 table-spoon vanilla frosting bright red. Clean and dry the paintbrush, and brush a thin layer of red frosting on the top and sides of 1 red Giant SweeTart. Poke a toothpick through the center of the frosted SweeTart, leaving ¼ inch exposed at the top. Push the toothpick into the center of the tuning dial to attach the SweeTart. Cut the large red gumdrop in half, and add it to the exposed toothpick, flat side against the SweeTart. Center 2 cherry Life Savers, 1½ inches apart, between the bottom of the radio and the tuning dial. Attach each of 2 red Dots to the cherry Life Savers with toothpicks. Position 6 evenly spaced purple jujubes on the tuning dial, and then pipe 2 small black dots between each pair of jujubes.

4 make the handle

Cut one of the 18-gauge wires in half with wire cutters. Wet one wire (to help it slide), and push the wire through a Strawberry Sour Punch Straw until the straw is centered on the wire. Pinch ½ inch of each end of the licorice straw between your thumb and index finger, and bend the ends 90 degrees. Repeat for the other wire and licorice straw. Centering both pieces of the handle together on the radio, gently push the wire ends into the cake until the tips of the licorice meet the surface of the cake. Put the curved sides of 2 red oval Jujyfruits against the handle ends. Pipe a black dot on top of the Jujyfruits where they connect to the handle.

5 make the antenna

Put 1 cherry Life Saver in the back left corner of the radio, between the back edge and the handle. Cut the remaining 18-gauge wire in half, and discard one half. Rub a small amount of black frosting onto the wire to color it gray. String the wire with 1 red Jujube, leaving 3 inches exposed on one end. Attach the red gumball to the top of the wire for the antenna, and curve the wire between the jujube and the gumball. Insert the exposed wire into the cake until the jujube rests on top of the Life Saver.

6 finish the radio

On the tuning dial, pipe a white line from the edge of the red gumdrop to the center. Pipe a white dot in the center of the gumdrop, followed by a black dot. Pipe white highlights on the radio, as seen in the photo.

game console

Remember those days when you couldn't wait to play your game console? With your hand on the joystick, you made frogs leap across the screen and blasted away alien invaders. This cake would be an awesome addition to an '80s theme party or surprise for someone who adores old-school technology. The game console will be instantly recognizable and a fun conversation piece.

SERVES 25 TO 30
LEVEL OF DIFFICULTY: 2.5

special tools

- 1 (13 × 19-inch) cake board
  Small offset spatula
- 1 (12-inch) cardboard cake circle
  1-inch flat-head paintbrush
- 2 (10-inch) wooden skewers
  Wire cutters

ingredients

- 1 (8 × 12-inch) sheet cake (¼ sheet) with vanilla or chocolate frosting
- 3 cups vanilla frosting (2 16-ounce cans)
- ¾ cup chocolate frosting (from 1 16-ounce can)
- 1 (16-ounce) frozen pound cake (we use Sara Lee family-size), thawed
- 1 (10.75-ounce) frozen pound cake (we use Sara Lee), thawed
- Paste or gel paste food coloring: black (SEE SOURCES, PAGE 201)
- 2 Giant Chewy SweeTarts, any color
- 1 large (2.25-ounce) Tootsie Roll (6 inches long)
- 4 Haribo Wheels, black licorice flavor
- 2 red Spree candies
- 1 red Mike and Ike candy, Original Fruits flavor

1 prepare the console cake

Remove the frosting decorations from the cake and trim the cake board (see pages 14 and 15). Put the cake, with its trimmed board, onto a 13 × 19-inch cake board, centering it ½ inch from the back edge. Glue it down.

In a medium bowl, mix 1½ cups vanilla frosting with ¾ cup chocolate frosting. Using a small offset spatula, frost the cake. Dip the spatula in hot water, shake off the excess, and carefully smooth the frosting. Clean up the board and refrigerate the cake.

2 make the wedge-shaped control panel

Lightly trim the top of the larger pound cake to make it flat. Lay the cake horizontally on your work surface, and using a chef's knife, score two lines along its full length, 1 inch from the bottom and top edges.

Stand the cake on a short end with the scored lines facing you. Line up the chef's knife on the top surface between the beginning of the left scored line and the top left corner on the same surface, and cut down following the scored line; discard the corner. Repeat on the right side. The trimmed cake should be a wedge with a flat top. Put the cake, wide side down, on a 12-inch round cardboard cake circle and refrigerate it.

3 make the controllers

Lightly trim the top of the smaller pound cake to make it flat, and remove the side crusts. Put the cake horizontally on your work surface, and cut off even amounts from both ends to make a 6 × 3-inch piece. Cut it in half to make 2 squares. Put the squares on separate plates and refrigerate.

4 frost the console, control panel, and controllers

In a bowl, tint ¾ cup vanilla frosting black. Make sure the sheet cake frosting is firm before proceeding, and work quickly but carefully through the following steps.

Using the 1-inch flat-head paintbrush, apply black frosting to just the top of the sheet cake, brushing lightly and evenly to fully cover the top. Dip an offset spatula in hot water, shake off the excess, and smooth the frosting. Refrigerate the cake.

Using the least amount of black frosting possible to achieve full coverage, frost the control panel with an offset spatula, and smooth the frosting. Clean up the cake circle and refrigerate the cake. Repeat the frosting and smoothing for the 2 controllers, and refrigerate.

5 assemble the console

Center the control panel ¼ inch from the back edge of the sheet cake. Fill a zip-top plastic bag with black frosting and cut ¼ inch off the tip. Pipe a border around each edge of the control panel, including the bottom. Pipe horizontal lines across the sheet cake, ¼ inch apart. Pipe the lines on both sides of the control panel, and a border around the

top and bottom of the sheet cake. Refrigerate.

Pipe a border around just the top of the 2 controllers, and refrigerate. For the joysticks, use a skewer to punch a hole in the center of each of the 2 Giant SweeTarts. Using the paintbrush, frost the top and sides of the SweeTarts black. Cut the Tootsie Roll in half and insert a skewer as far as possible into each piece without affecting the shape. Holding it by the skewer, brush each Tootsie Roll with black frosting. Put 1 black licorice wheel in the center of one controller, with the black frosted SweeTart on top. Using the wire cutters, cut off all but 2 inches of the skewer. Insert the skewer into the controller through the hole of the SweeTart. Set it aside and repeat for the second joystick.

Fill a plastic bag with the remainder of the brown frosting and cut ⅛ inch off the tip. Pipe 4 large dots, evenly spaced, around the licorice wheel on each controller and 4 small dots between the large dots. Put 1 red Spree in the upper left corner of each controller, and refrigerate.

6 decorate the console

Using the chocolate frosting, pipe a border around the front of the control panel. Cut 1 red Mike and Ike in half and put one half on the upper right side of the control panel. Using the bag of black frosting, pipe a 3 × 1½-inch box in the center of the panel, and three 1-inch-long vertical lines on each side.

In a bowl, tint 2 tablespoons vanilla frosting a light gray with black food coloring. Spoon it into a plastic bag and cut ⅛ inch off the tip. Pipe gray lines over the black lines just piped, and pipe a horizontal line over the vertical lines. Use the chocolate frosting to pipe dots around the gray lines as shown.

7 finish the console

Put the joystick controllers in front of the console. Make the cords by unraveling the remaining 2 black licorice wheels, and connect the joysticks to the back of the control panel.

jukebox

Rock around the clock with a vintage jukebox from the 1950s! This cake looks way more complicated than it really is because the decorations are so detailed. Once the colorful licorice twists and the rest of the candies are placed, it's just a matter of accenting the decorations with piped frosting and getting your cake groove on.

SERVES 40 TO 50

LEVEL OF DIFFICULTY: 2

special tools

- 1 (11½-inch) dinner plate
- 1 (13½ × 20½-inch) cake board
- Small offset spatula
- Small rolling pin
- 1 round toothpick

ingredients

- 1 (12 × 16-inch) sheet cake (½ sheet) with chocolate frosting
- 3¾ cups chocolate frosting (2½ 16-ounce cans)
- 1½ cups vanilla frosting (1 16-ounce can)
- Paste or gel paste food coloring: black (SEE SOURCES, PAGE 201)
- Cornstarch, for dusting
- 3 Tootsie Fruit Rolls: 1 green, 1 orange, and 1 pink
- 1 (5-ounce) package Haribo Wheels, black licorice flavor
- 3 large (2.25-ounce) Tootsie Rolls (each 6 inches long)
- 2 large (12.4-ounce) bags Twizzlers Rainbow Twists
- 1 (2-ounce) package Air Heads Xtremes Sweetly Sour Belts, Rainbow Berry flavor
- 4 crème wafer cookies (each 2½ inches long), strawberry flavor
- 1 rope Twizzlers Pull 'n' Peel, cherry flavor
- 3 large gumdrops: 2 yellow and 1 red
- 1 (1.5-ounce) box jujubes
- 2 Giant Chewy SweeTarts: 1 red and 1 green
- 1 tablespoon confetti sprinkles, rainbow color

1 prepare the cake

Remove the frosting decorations from the sheet cake (see page 14). To make the top arc, put the dinner plate facedown on the cake, with the edges meeting at the top center, and score a line around the top half of the plate. Remove the plate, cut along the line with a knife, and discard the trimmings. Trim the cake board (see page 15). Put the cake, on its trimmed board, on a 13 × 20½-inch cake board and attach with glue.

In a medium bowl, stir 2¼ cups chocolate frosting until smooth. Using an offset spatula, frost the cake. Dip the spatula in hot water, shake off the excess, and smooth the frosting. Clean up the cake board and refrigerate the cake.

In another bowl, tint ¾ cup vanilla frosting gray with black food coloring. Spoon the gray frosting into a zip-top plastic bag and cut ¼ inch off the tip; set aside. To make the piping more manageable, fill 2 more plastic bags with ½ cup chocolate frosting each, and cut ¼ inch off the tips; set aside.

2 make the records

Dust a work surface with cornstarch, and roll out, separately, the green, orange, and pink Tootsie Fruit Rolls. Using an empty plastic water bottle, stamp out 2 rounds each of green and orange, and 3 rounds of pink. Gently press each round onto the center of a licorice wheel, and punch a small hole in the middle of each with a toothpick. Set aside.

3 decorate the cake

Cut the large Tootsie Rolls in half and put them side-by-side on a clean work surface, in 2 groups of 3, lining up the indentations as much as possible. Use an offset spatula to make indentations straight across. Put the Tootsie Roll columns on the bottom left and right sides of the cake.

Put 3 green Twizzlers and 3 yellow Twizzlers on each side of the cake, touching the Tootsie Roll columns. Where the green Twizzlers end, add 3 red Twizzlers on each side, wrapping them around the top and filling in the gaps with pieces cut to fit. Repeat with the 3 orange Twizzlers, inside the red Twizzlers.

Using a reserved zip-top plastic bag of chocolate frosting, pipe 3 continuous borders—outer, inner, and middle—around the Twizzlers. Pipe a border around the 2 Tootsie Roll sections, and pipe vertical lines over the seams between them.

At the left seam where the red/orange and green/yellow Twizzlers meet, put 2 Sour Belts horizontally with the red stripes together. Cut them to fit so that they cover the piped borders and are anchored to the cake by the frosting. Repeat on the right side with 2 more Sour Belts.

Put the pink wafer cookies horizontally between the Sour Belts, lining them up end-to-end in 2 rows. At the top of the cake, just above the inner orange border, put 1 pink record in the center and attach it with gray frosting. Take a 3½-inch-long piece of blue Twizzler and cut it in half lengthwise. Angle the pieces against the pink record and attach them with chocolate frosting. Cut the ends at the top edge, just beyond the piped border.

Spoon ¼ cup vanilla frosting into a plastic bag and cut ⅛ inch off the tip. Leaving a ½-inch buffer on all sides, pipe a half-circle in the space above the pink wafer cookies and fill it in with thin horizontal lines. Smooth the frosting.

At the top of the jukebox, pipe 2 lines of gray frosting outside the blue Twizzlers, and connect the lines with a gray line below the record. Pipe gray borders around the outside of the white half-circle and the pink wafer cookies. Pipe a gray vertical line at the seam where the pink wafer cookies meet, and then every ¾ inch, until you have 3 vertical lines on each side. (Red licorice will be placed on the lines later.) Pipe a border around the two Sour Belt sections, and horizontally across the middle.

Pull 2 strands from the Twizzlers Pull 'n' Peel rope, line the inside of the half-circle, and cut to fit. On the pink wafer cookie section, put a piece of the red licorice strand on top of the gray lines, cutting each one to fit. Pipe gray lines in between the red licorice pieces.

4 make the speaker

Starting 2 inches below the wafer cookies and centered on the cake, put 4 blue Twizzlers in a U shape to form the speaker section. They should meet in the middle, 1½ inches from the bottom edge. Cut to fit. Using gray frosting, pipe a crosshatch design of evenly spaced lines inside the blue Twizzlers. Pipe 1 gray line across the top of the grid and a gray border around the outside of the blue licorice.

Put 2 red Pull 'n' Peel strands between the blue Twizzlers and cut to fit. Put 2 large yellow gumdrops at the top of the speaker and 1 red

gumdrop in the bottom half of the speaker grid. Pipe 3 small gray dots on the sides and top of each yellow gumdrop, and 4 small dots around the red gumdrop. Pipe a line down the bottom seam of the U shape and 2 across the sides.

5 continue decorating the jukebox

Put the colored jujubes on the cake as shown in the photo.

Cut 1 green and 1 red Giant SweeTart in half, and put one green half in the center above the pink wafer cookies and the other half on top of the speaker. Put the pink halves on either side of the green piece, as shown.

6 make the records in the window

Cut 3 licorice wheels in half. On 2 of the halves, remove 2 strands of licorice; on another 2 halves, remove 3 strands; and on the remaining 2 halves, remove 4 strands, creating the different-size records. Put the 2 largest records in the middle of the window, leaning slightly to the right, followed by the medium records on either side and then the smallest records, overlapping them as you go.

7 finish the cake

Using chocolate frosting, pipe 3 evenly spaced horizontal lines at the bottom of the jukebox. Scatter the remaining colored records, with 3 on the top and 3 on the bottom. Sprinkle edible confetti pieces around the cake.

FOR THE
betties

bustier

Perfect for a girls' night out or a bachelor party, this sexy pink bustier can play naughty or nice. It is one of the easiest recipes in the book and uses only four ingredients! We thought the pink and black was hot, but feel free to play with the color combinations to find what turns you on.

SERVES 15

LEVEL OF DIFFICULTY: 1

special tools

- 1 (9 × 13-inch) cake board
- Small offset spatula

ingredients

- 1 (8 × 12-inch) sheet cake (¼ sheet) with vanilla frosting
- 3 cups vanilla frosting (2 16-ounce cans)
- Paste or gel paste food coloring: pink and black (SEE SOURCES, PAGE 201)
- 8 Haribo Wheels, black licorice flavor

1 shape the cake

Remove the frosting decorations from the sheet cake (see page 14). Put the cake vertically on a work surface. Starting at the top edge of the cake, find the center, measure down 1½ inches, and make a mark. Measure in 2½ inches from the left and right corners on the top edge and make marks. Measure down 2 inches from the top left and right corners and make marks. Measure down 7 inches from the top of the cake

and score a line across (this is the waist of the bustier). Make a mark 1½ inches in from each side of the scored line. From the bottom edge of the cake, make a mark 2½ inches up from the left and right corners. Make a mark in the center of the bottom edge of the cake.

Using a sharp knife, score a line connecting all the marks around the perimeter of the cake to create the shape of the bustier. Cut through this scored line and discard the trimmings. Trim the cake board (see page 15). Put the cake, on its trimmed board, on a 9 × 13-inch cake board and attach with glue.

2 frost the cake

In a bowl, tint 2 cups vanilla frosting pink. Put ¼ cup pink frosting in a separate bowl for the crumb coat, and using an offset spatula, crumb-coat the cake with a thin layer. Clean up the board and refrigerate the cake until the frosting is firm, 20 to 25 minutes.

Frost the cake pink. Dip the spatula in hot water, shake off the excess, and smooth the frosting. Clean up the board and refrigerate the cake for 30 minutes.

Spoon ½ cup of the remaining pink frosting into a zip-top plastic bag (supplement if necessary), and cut ⅛ inch off the tip.

3 make the lace detail

Cut 6 black licorice wheels in half (it'll look best if you cut at the point where the licorice ends). Remove 2 of the outer rings from each half and set aside. Working from the outer edge toward the middle of

the bustier, place 3 halves on each side on the top and bottom. Cut the remaining 2 licorice wheels in half and remove 2 to 3 outer rings, depending on what fits. Put 2 of the halves on the top center and 1 on the bottom center.

Pipe a vertical line of pink frosting down the center of the cake. Following the photograph, pipe the curved lines around the bra and the 4 vertical lines outlining the contour of the bustier. Rotate the cake so that you are always piping from left to right, because you'll get cleaner lines than piping up and down. Pipe pink dots at the center of each wheel half, and a pink border around the base of the cake.

4 make the bow

Take 2 of the largest reserved licorice pieces, create a loop with each one, and press firmly at the tips to bind them together. Put them on the cake. Lay 2 more pieces on the cake as the tails of the bow.

In a bowl, tint 2 tablespoons vanilla frosting black. Spoon this into a zip-top plastic bag and cut ⅛ inch off the tip. Pipe a large dot in the middle of the bow and 5 evenly spaced "X" stitches, going over them again to thicken if necessary.

purse

A woman can never have too many purses, and this cute couture handbag cake is a must-have for any collection. Make sure to pay particular attention to the frosting process so you get as smooth a surface as possible—you use only a handful of candies for decorations, so you want to create the best backdrop to show them off. Also, take a good look at the photos on page 17 that demonstrate how to make the wedge shape.

SERVES 10 TO 12
LEVEL OF DIFFICULTY: 1.5

special tools

- 1 (5 × 10-inch) cake board
- **Large offset spatula**
- 1 (18- to 20-gauge) cloth- or paper-covered green or white wire, 18 inches long

ingredients

- 1½ cups vanilla frosting (1 16-ounce can)
- **Paste or gel paste food coloring: yellow and green** (SEE SOURCES, PAGE 201)
- 3 tablespoons chocolate frosting (from 1 16-ounce can)
- 3 (16-ounce) frozen pound cakes (we use Sara Lee family-size), thawed
- 2 (2-ounce) packages Sour Punch Straws, green apple flavor
- 1 Trolli Sour Apple-O's gummy candy
- 1 chocolate coin in gold foil
- 1 green Sixlet
- 2 green gumballs, regular size
- 1 Sour Punch Sip-n-Chew Candy Straw, Zappin' Apple flavor

1 prepare the frosting

In a bowl, tint the vanilla frosting an avocado green using a 2-to-1 ratio of yellow and green food coloring, and adding the chocolate frosting. Scoop ½ cup of the avocado frosting into a separate bowl for crumb-coating. Spoon 2 tablespoons of the frosting into a zip-top plastic bag and set aside.

2 shape the cake

Lightly trim the tops and sides of the pound cakes to make them flat, and reserve the trimmings. Stack the cakes on top of each other, applying a thin layer of the crumb-coat frosting between the layers. Cut equal amounts off the ends of the stack to make it 8½ inches long.

Using a chef's knife, score two lines along the length of the top of the stack, 1½ inches from the top and the bottom edges. Stand the stack on its short side with the lines facing you. Position the knife on the top between the beginning of the left scored line and the top left corner on the same surface. Cut down following the line, and discard the cut-off piece. Repeat on the right side. When done, the cake should resemble a wedge with a flat top. Put the cake, wide side down, on a 5 × 10-inch cake board and attach it with a small amount of frosting.

Fill in any gaps in the pound cake using the reserved cake trimmings, and crumb-coat the cake. Clean up the board and refrigerate until the frosting is firm, 15 to 20 minutes.

Using an offset spatula, frost the cake green. Dip the spatula in hot water, shake off the excess, and smooth the frosting. Clean up the board and refrigerate until firm, about 30 minutes.

3 decorate the purse

Cut two 5½-inch lengths of green Sour Punch Straws, and curve them from the top corners of the purse toward the center to make the flap detail. The strands should meet in the middle. Line all edges of the purse with Sour Punch Straws, cutting them to fit.

Cut ⅛ inch off the tip of the frosting bag. Pipe a ring of frosting on the white side of the Apple-O and attach it to the center of the gold coin. Attach the gold coin at the center of the flap detail just above the green straws. Squeeze a small dot of frosting inside the hole of the Apple-O and attach the green Sixlet.

4 add the handle

Holding the wire near the tip, poke it through the 2 gumballs, and then remove it. Insert the wire through the green Sour Punch Sip-n-Chew Candy Straw, leaving the ends evenly exposed. Measure 1½ inches in from the sides of the top of the cake to mark the ends of the purse handle. Bend the handle to line up with these marks. Thread the gumballs onto the ends of the wire, and then lightly push the handle into the cake.

stiletto

Fashionistas will go wild for this leopard-print stiletto with its pretty jeweled bow. Women adore their shoes, and Rick didn't take the responsibility of designing a stiletto cake lightly. Drawing inspiration from the runways and women's fashion magazines, the result was a sharp shoe that women would go crazy for. For less than the cost of a pair of shoes, you can feed 5 to 6 people with this cake and still have money left over to go shopping!

SERVES 5 TO 6
LEVEL OF DIFFICULTY: 2.5

special tools

1 (11 × 13-inch) cake board

Small offset spatula

#4 round artist's paintbrush

ingredients

1 (16-ounce) frozen pound cake (we use Sara Lee family-size), thawed

1½ cups vanilla frosting (1 16-ounce can)

½ cup chocolate frosting (from 1 16-ounce can)

Paste or gel paste food coloring: orange and black (SEE SOURCES, PAGE 201)

2 large (2.25-ounce) Tootsie Rolls (each 6 inches long)

2 sticks Wrigley's Doublemint gum

Liquid food coloring: black

Pure lemon extract

1 piece Nestle Sno-Caps Chocolate Nonpareils

1 shape the shoe

Lightly trim the top of the pound cake to make it flat. Position the cake vertically on a work surface, cut it in half lengthwise, and set aside one of the pieces. Position the other piece horizontally with the top side up and the rounded corners facing you. Measure 2½ inches from the right side and make a mark on the top edge. Line up the knife on the top surface between the mark and the bottom right corner on the same surface, and slice down (this will be the tall part of the shoe, not the toe). Set aside. Discard the cut-off piece.

Position the remaining cake piece for the toe horizontally with the top side up and the cut side toward you. Cut its length in half, and rotate the left piece 180 degrees counterclockwise. Relocate it so it lies horizontally and directly in front of the other piece, matching up the rounded edges. Consider the pieces as 1 cake. It should resemble half a pound cake as you look down on it. Cut off enough of the length from the left side to make the piece 4 inches long. Cut ¾ inch off its width. Discard the trimmings.

Take the set-aside cake pieces (the tall part of the shoe), and join the angled side to the left side of the piece just made. The pieces should fit together seamlessly and resemble the shoe part without the heel. Trim as needed. Make the tip of the shoe by measuring 1 inch in from the top right corner and cutting diagonally to remove the corner.

2 frost the shoe

In a bowl, tint 1½ cups vanilla frosting a light orange-brown with 3 tablespoons chocolate frosting and a little orange food coloring, added in small increments until you achieve a leopard color. Put ⅓ cup of this frosting in another bowl for crumb-coating. Center the cake pieces on the cake board, and using an offset spatula, attach the pieces to each

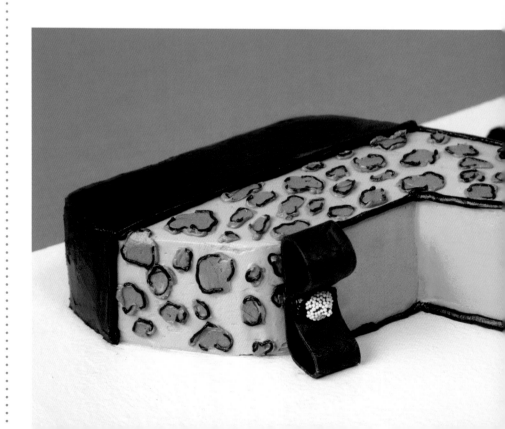

other and to the board with the crumb-coat frosting. Crumb-coat the cake. Clean up the board and refrigerate the cake until the frosting is firm, 15 to 20 minutes.

Frost the entire cake, and apply only a thin layer of frosting to the sole of the shoe (which will be frosted black). Dip the offset spatula in hot water, shake off the excess, and carefully smooth the frosting. Clean up the board and refrigerate the cake.

Put ⅓ cup of the leopard frosting into a bowl and tint it black with black paste or gel paste food coloring. Lightly frost the sole of the shoe without extending the frosting over the edge.

③ make the black platform of the shoe

Use the offset spatula to score a line across the shoe, 1½ inches from the bottom. Make sure the line extends around the front of the shoe to the board. Take half of the remaining black frosting and spoon it into a zip-top plastic bag. Cut ⅛ inch off the tip. Pipe a black line along the scored line and fill in the space with thin horizontal lines. Smooth the frosting. Clean up the board and refrigerate the cake.

④ make the heel

Smash the 2 large Tootsie Rolls together into a ball, and roll it into a conical shape that's 6½ to 7 inches long. Press the wide side of the cone into an angle that will fit flush with the sole of the shoe.

Position the heel, making sure the height and angle will properly align with the shoe. When the heel fits, push it into place. Lightly frost the heel with the remaining black frosting, and smooth. Clean up the board and refrigerate the cake until firm.

Starting at the top of the heel, pipe a thin black line down the edge of the shoe, straight across the black platform to the toe, and ending on the board. Pipe a black border around the inside of the shoe to where the bow will be placed.

⑤ make the leopard print

Take the remaining orange-brown frosting and mix it with an equal amount of chocolate frosting. Spoon this into a zip-top plastic bag and cut ⅛ inch off the tip. Pipe irregularly shaped and sized leopard-print dots all over the orange-brown frosting, first outlining the dot and then filling it in. Using the black frosting, partially outline the spots. Clean up the board and refrigerate the cake.

⑥ make the bow

Put the sticks of gum on wax paper. In a small bowl, mix ¼ teaspoon each of liquid black food coloring and lemon extract; brush this over the gum with a #4 paintbrush. Let dry for a few minutes; then paint the other side. When the color is dry, fold the gum sticks over, creating loops, and put the first loop closest to the cake board. Contour the loop by slightly flattening the side where it touches the board. Attach the second loop to the other side, gently pressing the whole bow into the cake. To finish it, pipe a black dot the size of a chickpea on the top center and lightly press a Sno-Cap into it.

makeup bag

Wondering what to give a makeup enthusiast for her birthday? More makeup, of course! All handmade and spilling out of a stylish edible makeup case. The makeup bag is shaped using a wedge-cut technique like that used in the purse recipe (page 97). This beauty-full cake has all the essentials and will get you ready for a night on the town.

makeup bag

SERVES 10 TO 12
LEVEL OF DIFFICULTY: 2

special tools

- 1 (9 × 13-inch) cake board
- Small offset spatula
- ½-inch flat-head paintbrush
- #4 round artist's paintbrush
- 1 (10-inch) wooden skewer
- Wire cutters
- 1 round toothpick

ingredients

- 3 (10.75-ounce) frozen pound cakes (we use Sara Lee), thawed
- 3 cups of vanilla frosting (2 16-ounce cans)
- Paste or gel paste food coloring: black (SEE SOURCES, PAGE 201)
- 1 roll Hubba Bubba Bubble Tape, green apple flavor
- Liquid food coloring: black
- Pure lemon extract
- 6 sticks Wrigley's Doublemint gum
- 1 (1.4-ounce) York Peppermint Pattie
- ½ teaspoon chocolate frosting (from 1 16-ounce can)
- 2 Giant Chewy SweeTarts: 1 green and 1 purple
- 2 large gumdrops: 1 yellow and 1 orange
- 1 large (2.25-ounce) Tootsie Roll (6 inches long)
- 1 black Twizzler
- 1 chocolate Tootsie Roll Midgee
- 2 vanilla Tootsie Roll Midgees
- 2 red Jolly Rancher Fruit Chews
- 6 pink Starburst candies

1 shape the cake

Trim the tops off 2 of the pound cakes to make them completely flat. Stack all 3 cakes horizontally with the untrimmed cake on top, applying a thin layer of vanilla frosting between the layers as "glue." Cut the stack into a wedge shape: Using a chef's knife, score two lines along the length of the top of the stack, 1 inch from the top and bottom edges. Stand the stack on its short side with the scored lines facing you. Position the knife on the top surface between the beginning of the right scored line and the top right corner on the same surface, and cut through. Discard the cut-off piece. Repeat on the left side.

Lay the stack on your work surface with the tapered side facing you. On the farthest edge, measure 1 inch in from each side and make a mark. Line up the knife on the top surface between the bottom right corner and the right scored mark, and cut through; discard the cut-off corner. Repeat on the left side. The cake should now resemble the tapered wedge shape of the makeup bag.

In a bowl, tint 1¼ cups vanilla frosting gray with black food coloring, and spoon ½ cup into another bowl for crumb-coating. Center the cake on the cake board with the bottom of the bag 1 inch from the bottom edge. Attach it with a small amount of frosting. Using an offset spatula, crumb-coat the cake. Clean up the board and refrigerate the cake until the frosting is firm, 15 to 20 minutes. Then frost the cake with gray frosting. Dip the spatula in hot water, shake off the excess, and carefully smooth the frosting.

2 decorate the makeup bag

Cut a 20-inch piece of the Hubba Bubba Bubble Tape and put it on a piece of wax paper. Mix ½ teaspoon each of liquid black food coloring and lemon extract. Using a ½-inch flat-head paintbrush, stain the top of the Bubble Tape black. Let dry.

Turn the cake board around so the top opening of the bag is facing you. Starting ½ inch above the bottom right corner, put 1 stick of the Wrigley's Doublemint gum on the top at about a 45-degree angle, and cut to fit. Line up the remaining sticks of gum end-to-end in 2 parallel rows spaced ¾ inch apart; cut to fit.

Starting at the top left corner, run the black strip of Bubble Tape across the white stripes, ending ½ inch left of the bottom right corner; cut to fit. Put the next 2 rows of parallel black strips ¾ inch apart below the first strip, and cut to fit. Use the #4 paintbrush to dab water under the black strips where they cross the white strips to make them stick.

Spoon ¼ cup of the remaining gray frosting into a zip-top plastic bag and cut ¼ inch off the tip. Pipe an angled line 1½ inches above and parallel to the black strips. In a bowl, tint ¼ cup vanilla frosting black. Spoon into a plastic bag and cut ¼ inch off the tip. Pipe a black outline around all edges of the makeup bag except for the short ends at the top, where the bag opens. At these open corners, pipe a "V."

Pipe a gray line down each side of the bag, from the bottom of the black "V" to the bottom of the bag. Set the cake aside but do not refrigerate, because the coloring on the black strips could run.

3 make the makeup

Prepare an 8-inch piece of wax paper to put the makeup items on as you are working. Keep in mind that after you touch a tinted black makeup piece, you should wash your hands before touching a colored piece.

To make the powder compact, squeeze half of the black frosting from the bag into a bowl. Using a clean ½-inch flat-head paintbrush, brush the bottom and sides of the Peppermint Pattie black. Set aside, frosted side up.

In a bowl, mix 2 tablespoons vanilla frosting with ½ teaspoon chocolate frosting. Spoon this into a zip-top plastic bag and cut ⅛ inch off the tip. On the frosted side of the Peppermint Pattie, pipe a brown circle ½ inch from the edge and fill it in. Smooth the frosting. Pipe a black outline around the brown center. Trim ½ inch from one side of the compact so that it will lie flush against the makeup bag. Set aside.

To make the eye shadows, use the flat-head paintbrush to brush black frosting on the tops and sides of the Giant Chewy SweeTarts. Cut one-third off the flat side of the yellow and orange gumdrops, and discard the rounded parts. Put the cut pieces, sugared side up, on the centers of the frosted SweeTarts. Set aside.

To make the lipstick tube, cut off a 4-segment piece of the large Tootsie Roll and brush it with the black frosting. Set aside.

To make the mascara, cut a 2-segment piece of large Tootsie Roll. Roll it between your hands until it is 2 inches long. Set aside. Cut 1¼ inches off the end of the black Twizzler. Using a wire cutter, cut 4 inches off the pointed end of the wooden skewer, and discard the rest. Insert the pointed end of the skewer into the Twizzler piece and the other end ½ inch into the Tootsie Roll. Brush the Tootsie Roll handle with black frosting, and set aside.

To make the makeup brush handle, take the remaining Tootsie Roll segments and roll them between your hands to form a piece 3 inches long and slightly conical. Brush it with black frosting and set aside.

4 assemble the makeup pieces

Position the makeup bag with the top of the bag facing you. Put the compact flush with the bag, 2 inches from the right side. Put the makeup brush handle at an angle to the right of the compact. Smash together 1 chocolate Tootsie Roll Midgee and 1 vanilla Tootsie Roll Midgee to form a 1-inch piece with one end tapered to fit the top of the brush handle. Press the blade of an offset spatula into the piece to make bristle indentations.

Put the lipstick tube at an angle between the makeup brush and the powder compact. Smash together the red Jolly Rancher Fruit Chews, form them into a 1½-inch-long tube, and flatten one side to resemble lipstick. Put this at the end of the tube. Pipe a gray border where the colored piece meets the handle on the makeup brush and on the lipstick.

Put the mascara wand at an opposite angle to the makeup brush, 2 inches from the left side of the bag. Pipe a gray line over the skewer on the mascara wand. Put the orange eye shadow between the mascara and the compact, and the yellow eye shadow against the mascara handle.

Smash together 6 pink Starbursts and roll them between your hands to form a 1¼-inch-long log. Shape it into the bottom of a nail polish bottle. Cut a toothpick in half, and stick one half into a vanilla Tootsie Roll Midgee and the other half into the nail polish bottle. Put the nail polish bottle on the board with the top against the mascara wand.

gift box of pearls

Sometimes the best gifts are made at home and come in the smallest packages. This endearing cake is so pretty and realistic, it may be hard to eat! With white gumballs masquerading as pearls, you can achieve a luxe look without breaking the bank.

SERVES 2

LEVEL OF DIFFICULTY: 2

special tools

- 1 (18- to 22-gauge) silver wire, 18 inches long
- 1 (6-inch) cardboard cake circle covered in grease-resistant wrapping paper
- Small offset spatula

ingredients

- 18 white gumballs, regular size
- 2 (10.75-ounce) frozen pound cakes (we use Sara Lee), thawed
- 1½ cups vanilla frosting (1 16-ounce can)
- Paste or gel paste food coloring: blue and green (SEE SOURCES, PAGE 201)
- 17 sticks Wrigley's Doublemint gum
- ¼ cup white chocolate melting wafers (SEE SOURCES, PAGE 201)
- 1 large white gumdrop
- 1 white Necco wafer

1 make the strand of pearls

Bend one end of the silver wire to prevent the gumballs from falling off. Start the hole on each gumball with a safety pin and then thread them onto the wire. Once the gumballs are strung, leaving even amounts of the wires exposed, twist the ends together to form a bracelet. Set aside.

2 make the gift box

Lightly trim the tops of the pound cakes to make them completely flat, and remove the side crusts. Cut off equal amounts from each end to reduce the length to 6 inches. Cut both loaves in half so that you have four 3 × 3-inch pieces. Discard 1 piece.

In a bowl, tint the vanilla frosting turquoise blue, starting with blue food coloring and gradually adding a touch of green. Scoop ¼ cup of the frosting into another bowl for crumb-coating, and use it to attach one of the cake squares to the center of a 6-inch cardboard cake circle covered in grease-resistant paper. Stack the second cake on the first, attaching it with a little frosting. Set aside the third cake piece; it will become the lid.

Drape the pearl bracelet on the edge of the gift box and bend it so that 2 pearls lie in the mouth of the box and the rest falls naturally. The bottom should touch the cake board to help support its weight. (Positioning the bracelet in advance avoids damage to the box when you finally place it in Step 3.) Remove the bracelet and set aside.

Using an offset spatula, crumb-coat the cake. Clean up the cake circle and refrigerate the cake until the frosting is firm, 15 to 20 minutes.

Turn the remaining cake square on its side and cut its thickness in half; discard one of the halves. Attach the remaining piece to a plate with frosting, and crumb-coat it. Clean up the plate and refrigerate until firm, about 15 minutes.

Working with one cake at a time, take them out of the refrigerator and frost them. Dip a spatula in hot water, shake off the excess, and carefully smooth the frosting. Clean up the cake circle and plate, and refrigerate the cakes until firm, about 30 minutes.

3 decorate the cake

Take the larger cake, and put 1 stick of gum vertically in the center of each side. If the gum doesn't reach the top edge, use another stick and cut each piece to fit.

Spoon the remaining turquoise frosting into a zip-top plastic bag and cut ¼ inch off the tip. Pipe a border around the bottom of the box. Position the pearl bracelet on the box as before. Bend the excess wire and insert it into the cake. Refrigerate.

4 finish the box top

Take the small cake, put 1 stick of gum on each side flush with the bottom center, and drape it over the lid. All the sticks of gum should meet in the middle but not overlap; cut to fit.

In a microwave-safe bowl, melt the white chocolate wafers at 10-second intervals, stirring until smooth. Spoon the melted white chocolate into a zip-top plastic bag, and cut ⅛ inch off the tip. Take 5 sticks of gum and fold each one to make a loop. Cut off the corners to form a point. Attach the points of each loop together with a little melted chocolate.

Evenly space the ribbon loops on top of the lid to form a flower shape with all the points meeting in the center. Secure the points to the lid with a little melted chocolate. Cut the bottom third off the white gumdrop and discard the rounded top. Using the melted chocolate, attach it, cut side up, to the middle of the bow, and then attach the Necco wafer, printed side down, to the gumdrop.

Cut 2 sticks of gum in half. Cut out a triangle on one end of each stick, and cut the other end to a point. Put the points toward the bow at the four corners of the lid. Refrigerate until the frosting is firm, about 30 minutes.

5 assemble the box

Squeeze a dollop of turquoise frosting onto the top center of the box. The frosting should be higher than the pearls, so that when the lid is placed on top, the frosting won't squeeze out the sides. Carefully place the lid on top, resting on the pearls.

NO
passport
REQUIRED

double–decker bus

LONDON

During the time Rick was designing projects for this book, he was invited to teach in London and was very excited about it—"chuffed to bits," as they say. So London was on our minds while working on the travel chapter, and we knew the iconic double-decker bus would make a fantastic cake. The Union Jack flag in the background gives the cake the right spirit and makes for a striking design.

SERVES 20 TO 25
LEVEL OF DIFFICULTY: 3.5

special tools

- 1 (9 × 13-inch) cake board
  Small offset spatula
- 2 (10-inch) cardboard cake circles
  ½-inch flat-head paintbrush

ingredients

- 1 (8 × 12-inch) sheet cake (¼ sheet) with vanilla frosting
- 3¾ cups vanilla frosting (2½ 16-ounce cans)
- 1 (10.75-ounce) frozen pound cake (we use Sara Lee), thawed
  Paste or gel paste food coloring: red, blue, and black (SEE SOURCES, PAGE 201)
- 1 Fruit by the Foot, strawberry flavor
- 3 Giant Chewy SweeTarts, any color
- 1 rope Twizzlers Pull 'n' Peel, cherry flavor
- 1 Haribo Wheel, strawberry flavor
- 2 (2-ounce) packages Sour Punch Straws, strawberry flavor

① prepare the cake

Remove the frosting decorations from the cake and trim the cake board (see pages 14 and 15). Put the cake, on its trimmed board, on a 9 × 13-inch cake board and attach with glue.

In a medium bowl, stir 1½ cups vanilla frosting until smooth. Using an offset spatula, frost the cake. Dip the spatula in hot water, shake off the excess, and carefully smooth the frosting. Clean up the board and refrigerate the cake.

② make the bus

Lightly trim the top of the pound cake to make it flat. Flip the pound cake on its side and cut its thickness in half. Cut one of the pieces in half lengthwise and discard the other half. Lay the larger piece horizontally, and put the smaller piece just above it, cut edge flush against the large piece. The cakes should resemble the general shape of the bus. At the top left and right corners, measure in ½ inch diagonally and trim the corners, rounding them off. At the bottom left corner, measure 1 inch up and cut out a notch 1 inch high and ¼ inch wide to create the front window.

In a bowl, tint ½ cup of vanilla frosting red. Scoop 2 tablespoons into a separate bowl for crumb-coating. Attach the cake pieces to each other and to a 10-inch cardboard cake circle with a thin layer of frosting. Using scissors, trim the excess cardboard around the perimeter of the cake, including the notch, and put the cake, on the trimmed board, onto another 10-inch cardboard cake circle. Crumb-coat the cake with the red

frosting, using an offset spatula. Clean up the cake circle, and refrigerate the cake until the frosting is firm, 15 to 20 minutes. Then frost the cake red. Dip the spatula in hot water, shake off the excess, and carefully smooth the frosting. Clean up the cake circle and refrigerate.

③ frost the union jack flag

Unravel the Fruit by the Foot and use it to create a cross on the sheet cake, cutting with scissors to fit. Using a knife, cut the remaining piece of Fruit by the Foot in half, and then cut the width of those pieces in half, making 4 thin strips.

Starting at the lower right, slightly offset from the corner, run 1 thin red strip to meet the cross in the middle. Don't worry if the piece is too short because the bus will cover it. Repeat with the 3 remaining strips on the other corners.

Keeping the bus attached to the trimmed cardboard, center it on the sheet cake with the notch facing left, repairing any damage to the frosting with an offset spatula dipped in hot water.

In a bowl, tint ⅓ cup vanilla frosting blue. Spoon this into a zip-top plastic bag and cut ⅛ inch off the tip. Pipe the outlines of the blue sections of the flag, using the photo as a guide. Fill in the blue sections by piping thin horizontal lines back and forth, and then smooth the frosting.

④ decorate the bus

In a bowl, tint ⅓ cup vanilla frosting gray with black food coloring. Spoon it into a zip-top plastic bag and cut ⅛ inch off the tip. Starting at the driver's window, pipe the outline, ¾ inch wide by 1 inch high. Moving ¾ inch to the right, pipe a 2¼-inch-wide by 1-inch-high window. Move ½ inch to the right and pipe the third window with the same dimensions. The top deck windows are all 1 inch below the top of the bus. Starting ¼ inch from the left, pipe evenly spaced windows 1½ inches wide by ¾ inch high. Carefully fill in each window by piping thin horizontal lines, and smooth the frosting.

Squeeze the remaining gray frosting from the bag into a bowl and tint it black. Lay down a piece of wax paper. To make the bus wheels, take the 3 Giant SweeTarts and cut 1 in half. Using a ½-inch flat-head paintbrush, brush the wheels with a thin coat of black frosting; set aside on the wax paper.

Put the 2 whole wheels on the bus hanging halfway off the cake. Put the 2 half wheels under the bus, lined up with the others. Unravel a strand of Pull 'n' Peel licorice and lay it down the length of the bus, halfway between the two window sections, and cut to fit. Take 1 red licorice wheel and cut it in half. Peel off the outer ring of each half and put them over the tops of the wheels.

Spoon the black frosting into a plastic bag and cut ⅛ inch off the tip. Pipe all the black outlines on the flag and around the surface of the bus. Pipe 1 line across the top above the windows, and outline each window.

Spoon 2 tablespoons vanilla frosting into a plastic bag and cut ⅛ inch off the tip. Pipe an "L" inside the left corner of each

window and a horizontal line above the red Pull 'n' Peel. Pipe 1 headlight on the front of the bus. Squeeze the vanilla frosting into a bowl and tint it gray with black food coloring. Spoon it into a plastic bag and cut ⅛ inch off the tip. Pipe a dime-size circle on the center of the wheels, and 1 larger dot in the middle with 5 small dots around it. Pipe a border around the headlight.

⑤ finish the cake

Attach the red Sour Punch Straws as a border around the edges of the sheet cake, cutting to fit.

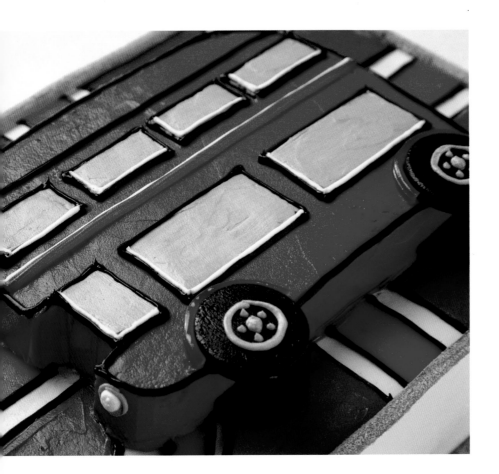

day *of the* dead
MEXICO

In Mexico, *Día de los Muertos,* or Day of the Dead, is a two-day holiday in November, when loved ones who have passed away are honored and celebrated. Traditions during the Day of the Dead include building altars and placing gifts of sugar skulls and favorite foods for the deceased on them. It is a celebration of abundance and color, and is the inspiration for this cake.

SERVES 20 TO 25

LEVEL OF DIFFICULTY: 2

special tools

- 1 (10 × 14-inch) cake board
- Small offset spatula
- 2 (10-inch) cardboard cake circles

ingredients

- 1 (8 × 12-inch) sheet cake (¼ sheet) with vanilla frosting
- 3 cups vanilla frosting (2 16-ounce cans)
- 1 (16-ounce) frozen pound cake (we use Sara Lee family-size), thawed
- 2 yellow Giant Chewy SweeTarts (from 2 [1.5-ounce] packages)
- 1 (1.7-ounce) package Chewy Spree candies
- 2 Life Savers, peppermint flavor
- 9 strands Twizzlers Pull 'n' Peel, cherry flavor
- 1 (.5-ounce) package Necco Candy Buttons
- 8 pieces Trident White gum
- 2 large orange gumdrops
- Paste or gel paste food coloring: black (SEE SOURCES, PAGE 201)
- 1 small (.74-ounce) candy necklace
- 1 large (1.4-ounce) candy necklace
- 8 Nerds Ropes, Rainbow flavor
- 4 Trolli Sour Apple-O's
- 4 pieces Jelly Belly Raspberries & Blackberries, blackberry flavor
- 1 (6-ounce) box Mike and Ike, Original Fruits flavor
- 22 gumballs, regular size, assorted colors

1 prepare the cake

Remove the frosting decorations from the cake and trim the cake board (see pages 14 and 15). Put the cake, on its trimmed board, on a 10 × 14-inch cake board and attach with glue.

In a medium bowl, stir 1½ cups vanilla frosting until smooth. Using an offset spatula, frost the cake. Dip the spatula in hot water, shake off the excess, and carefully smooth the frosting. Clean up the board and refrigerate the cake.

2 make the skull

Lightly trim the top of the pound cake to make it flat. Flip the cake on its side and cut the thickness in half. Lay the 2 halves together vertically on a work surface. Cut equal amounts off the left and right sides to make a combined cake 5 inches wide.

Turn the pieces horizontally, and attach them with a small amount of frosting. Cut ½ inch off both the left and the right side of the cake, and save the left-hand trimming. Cut another 2½ inches off the right side; this will form the jaw. The large piece is the head and should be 6 inches wide. Trim the jaw piece to 2½ by 4 inches, discard the trimmings, and center it under the head.

Take the reserved ½-inch strip and put its cut side against the top of the head, centered horizontally. At the top left and right corners of the cake, measure in ¼ inch diagonally toward the center and trim the corners, rounding them off to form the skull.

In a medium bowl, stir 1 cup vanilla frosting until smooth, and scoop ¼ cup into a separate bowl for crumb-coating. Attach the jaw

and the horizontal strip to the skull, and then attach the skull to a 10-inch cardboard cake circle with a little frosting. Using scissors, trim off the excess cardboard around the cake. Put the cake, with its cut cardboard, onto another 10-inch cardboard cake circle. Crumb-coat the cake with a thin layer of frosting. Clean up the cake circle and refrigerate the cake until the frosting is firm, about 15 minutes.

Using an offset spatula, frost the skull cake with the vanilla frosting. Dip the spatula in hot water, shake off the excess, and carefully smooth the frosting. Clean up the cake circle and refrigerate until firm, 20 to 25 minutes.

Keeping the cut cardboard piece attached to the skull cake, carefully center the skull vertically on the sheet cake, using your hand and an offset spatula.

3 decorate the skull

For the eyes, put 2 yellow Giant SweeTarts 2½ inches from the top of the skull and ¾ inch apart. Push the SweeTarts into the cake to make the frosting rise around them, forming an outline. Cut 3 yellow, 2 orange, and 2 red Chewy Sprees in half and arrange them around the eyes. Put 2 peppermint Life Savers on the yellow SweeTarts and attach them with frosting. Cut two 5¼-inch-long strands of Twizzlers Pull 'n' Peel and wrap them around the yellow eyes, staying inside the white outline, cutting to fit. Put blue Necco Candy Buttons around the red licorice.

To make the nose, cut 1 green Chewy Spree in half and position the halves, rounded sides up. Make a border around the top edge of the skull with a strand of Twizzlers Pull 'n' Peel and cut to fit.

To make the teeth, put 8 evenly spaced pieces of Trident White gum in 2 rows of 4. Outline the mouth and between the teeth with a Pull 'n' Peel strand, cutting to fit. Put 20 pink Necco Candy Buttons, evenly spaced, around the mouth. Cut the thickness of 2 large orange gumdrops in half, and put the domed halves on the cheeks.

In a bowl, tint ¼ cup vanilla frosting black. Spoon this into a zip-top plastic bag and cut ⅛ inch off the tip. Pipe black dots between the pink candies around the mouth.

Pipe an outline around the Chewy Sprees on the eyes and a small dot for the pupils. Pipe curved lines on the forehead, as shown in the photo.

Break open the small and large candy necklaces and put the pieces in a bowl. Put 2 yellow pieces under the green nose for the nostrils. Reserving the blue necklace pieces, put the candies, in alternating colors, in the eyebrow and forehead areas, as shown in the photo. Pipe small black dots on the forehead pieces and the

nostrils. Put 2 yellow Necco buttons on the black dots on the nostrils. Cut 1 yellow and 1 red Chewy Spree in half. Arrange 2 yellow halves and 1 red half, rounded side up, at the center of the piped curved lines on the forehead.

④ decorate the sheet cake

Use the Nerds Ropes to make a border around both the top and the base of the sheet cake, cutting to fit. Put 1 green Apple-O on each of the 4 corners of the cake and 1 blackberry-shaped Jelly Belly in the center of each Apple-O; then put 3 pink Necco buttons on top. For each corner, cut 1 yellow and 1 orange Mike and Ike candy in half, and stand the halves, evenly spaced, around the Apple-O. Put 2 blue and 1 red candy necklace pieces between the Mike and Ike pieces and pipe a black dot in the center of each.

Evenly space 22 gumballs inside the border: 4 on the top and bottom and 7 on each side, leaving room for yellow Necco Candy Buttons in between.

volcano
HAWAII

We live in the state of Hawaii, which is home to Kilauea, one of the world's most active volcanoes. This volcano cake is one of the most adventurous projects in the book, so take your time assembling the cakes and doughnuts and sculpting the conical shape. Remember not to smooth out the frosting too much—the imperfections make for a more realistic scene.

SERVES 25
LEVEL OF DIFFICULTY: 4

special tools

1 (14 × 21-inch) cake board

8 drinking straws

1 (8-inch) cardboard cake circle

Small offset spatula

3 (22- to 26-gauge) cloth- or paper-covered wires, 18 inches long

Wire cutters

#4 artist's paintbrush

3 (10-inch) wooden skewers

ingredients

5¼ cups vanilla frosting (3½ 16-ounce cans)

3 cups chocolate frosting (2 16-ounce cans)

1 angel food cake measuring 8½ inches across the top

1 bakery ring cake (6½ to 7 inches)

4 plain small doughnuts (from a 12-count box; each about 2¼ inches in diameter)

3 glazed old-fashioned doughnuts (from a 6-count box; each about 3¼ inches in diameter)

1 (11-ounce) box Little Debbie Coffee Cakes, Apple Streusel flavor

Paste or gel paste food coloring: green, blue, and red (SEE SOURCES, PAGE 201)

¾ cup ground vanilla wafers

¼ cup granulated sugar

1 individual vanilla pudding cup

12 sticks Wrigley's Spearmint gum

½ cup white chocolate melting wafers (SEE SOURCES, PAGE 201)

Pure lemon extract

Liquid food coloring: green

2 Pepperidge Farm Crème Filled Pirouette Rolled Wafers, chocolate flavor

4 brown Sixlets

1 build the volcano

In a bowl, mix 2¼ cups vanilla frosting with ½ cup chocolate frosting to make a light brown color.

Put a 14 × 21-inch cake board horizontally on your work surface. Put the angel food cake, wide base down, on the board, 3 inches from the right side and centered. To create the support structure for the volcano, push 8 drinking straws, evenly spaced, through the cake to the board, and use scissors to cut each straw level with the top of the cake.

Using a serrated knife, cut off the top of the ring cake to make it completely flat, setting the top aside. Before stacking them, measure the diameter of the ring cake and the top of the angel food cake to make sure they match up. Trim where necessary.

Set the ring cake on an 8-inch cardboard cake circle and attach it with a little frosting. Cut away the excess cardboard with scissors so the board is flush with the ring. Put the ring cake on top of the angel food cake, using a little frosting to attach it.

To extend the conical shape, you will sculpt the ring cake to the same angle as the angel food cake: Using a skewer, score an inner ring on the top of the ring cake, ½ inch from the outer edge. Cut away the sides of the cake at an angle from the scored line to the bottom edge of the cake, reserving the trimmings. Squish 2 small doughnuts into the center opening to fill the ring cake.

The next layer of the volcano is built with doughnuts: Center 1 large doughnut on top of the cake. Cut 3 small doughnuts in half, creating arches. Arrange the

build your cake like this

arches, cut side down, around the doughnut, and then attach them with frosting. Using a serrated knife, trim the doughnuts at an angle so that they are in line with the cakes below. Attach 1 large doughnut on top with frosting, and trim the excess. Repeat with another large doughnut. Break up a small doughnut and use it to fill most of the hole in the top doughnut, leaving a ½-inch-deep crater.

Crumb-coat the cake with a thin layer of the light brown frosting, filling in any gaps to create a smooth conical surface.

2 make the island details

Begin with the front part of the island: Unwrap 6 of the Little Debbie Coffee Cakes. Flip 3 of the cakes onto their long sides and cut their thickness in half. Rotate the cake board vertically so the volcano is farthest from you. Put 1 uncut coffee cake, streusel side down, in front of the volcano, and 2 more on either side of it, flush against the volcano. You are laying the groundwork for the palm trees.

Take the cut coffee cake pieces and put one in the center, in front of the first piece, cut side up. Put 2 more cut pieces on either side of the center as before. In the same manner, use 2 cut pieces to create a third row centered in front of the second. Cut the length of the last cake piece in half and put one half on each end of the row closest to the volcano.

Take the reserved top of the ring cake and cut it into 2 half-circles. Put them at the back of the volcano with the cut sides against it. Use the reserved ring cake trimmings to fill in the space and create a transition from the inner row to the outer row. This will make the area thick enough to anchor the palm trees. Use the remaining cake trimmings to fill in the gaps.

Crumb-coat the island with the light brown frosting. Smooth all the cake pieces to look like one island, eliminating all right angles. The end result should be an island with a slightly irregular oval shape. Refrigerate the cake until the frosting is firm, about 45 minutes.

3 frost the volcano and island

In a medium bowl, stir 1½ cups chocolate frosting until smooth, and frost the volcano. For a realistic look, the frosted surface should show some texture and not be perfectly smooth. When frosting the top of the volcano, fill most of the opening, but leave an indentation for the lava.

In a small bowl, tint 1 cup vanilla frosting light green with green food coloring. Using a small offset spatula, frost a thin green layer around the volcano, spreading it farther in the front than on the sides and back. Leave the area around the edge of the island unfrosted for the sand.

In another bowl, using your hands, combine the ground vanilla wafers and sugar. Scatter the mixture around the island in the unfrosted area. Wipe down the cake board. Add more green food coloring to the bowl of green frosting to make a darker shade. Spoon the frosting into a zip-top plastic bag and cut 1/16 inch (slightly larger than a pinhole) off the tip. Cover the green frosting with squiggly lines of the darker green to make grass.

In a separate bowl, tint 1½ cups vanilla frosting ocean blue with blue food coloring. Spread it over the board with wavy strokes. In another bowl, stir ¼ cup vanilla frosting until smooth. Using a clean spatula, frost the tops of the waves randomly to look like foam.

4 add the lava

In a bowl, mix the vanilla pudding with red food coloring to achieve a bright red. Using the offset spatula, lightly etch canals over the front of the volcano, from the top down. Spoon the red pudding into a zip-top plastic bag and cut ¼ inch off the tip. Squeeze the pudding into the canal lines, and add more in the opening at the top.

5 make the palm trees

Cut the sticks of gum into wide leaves, preserving the length and width. Put the leaves on a piece of wax paper. Cut the wire into twelve 4-inch-long pieces with wire cutters. Wash and dry a frosting can to hold the trees as you work.

In a microwave-safe bowl, melt the white chocolate wafers at 10-second intervals, stirring until smooth. Spoon the melted chocolate into a zip-top plastic bag and cut ¼ inch off the tip. Starting from a position two-thirds from the base of a gum leaf, pipe a line down the middle to the base. Attach one of the wires to the piped line, and gently secure it to the leaf. Lightly smooth the chocolate with your finger. Repeat for the other leaves and wires.

In a small bowl, mix 2 teaspoons lemon extract with 1 teaspoon liquid green food coloring. Gripping the wire where it meets the leaf, use a paintbrush to brush both sides of each leaf. Put the painted leaves on wax paper for 15 minutes to dry. Using scissors, make 4 cuts on the sides of each leaf.

Take 3 leaves, pinch them at the base, bend the wire 90 degrees, and use your fingers to gently shape each leaf. Do not bend the leaves too much or they will break. Stick the 3 leaves, evenly spaced, into a Pirouette wafer. Take 3 more leaves, bend the wire 45 degrees, shape them, and stick them, evenly spaced, into the same wafer. Repeat for the other palm tree.

To create the support for a palm tree, stick 1 wooden skewer through the bottom of the wafer and cut it flush with the bottom of the trunk. Spoon ¼ cup chocolate frosting into a plastic bag and cut ⅛ inch off the tip. To create the coconuts, attach 2 brown Sixlets to the top of the trunk with the chocolate frosting. Repeat for the second palm tree. Set the trees in the empty frosting can until you are ready to present the cake.

To attach the trees, place them, one at a time, 1½ inches apart in the grass, leaning slightly away from each other. (If placed at too much of an angle, the trees could fall over.) Gently push them down to the cake board to secure them.

dutch windmill

We have always wanted to visit the Netherlands. Until we're able to travel there, we can celebrate it with this cake. We were inspired by Holland's legendary tulips and the picturesque windmills that dot the countryside. To help create the shape of the windmill and make it as realistic as possible, we've included a diagram.

SERVES 50
LEVEL OF DIFFICULTY: 3.5

special tools

Small offset spatula

1 (13 × 19-inch) cake board

1 (10-inch) cardboard cake circle

1-inch flat-head paintbrush

4 (10-inch) wooden skewers

Wire cutters

½-inch flat-head paintbrush

1 drinking straw

ingredients

1 (12 × 16-inch) sheet cake (½ sheet) with vanilla frosting

6 cups vanilla frosting (4 16-ounce cans)

1 (16-ounce) frozen pound cake (we use Sara Lee family-size), thawed

1 (10.75-ounce) frozen pound cake (we use Sara Lee), thawed

½ cup chocolate frosting (from 1 16-ounce can)

2 Post Shredded Wheat Original biscuits

Paste or gel paste food coloring: blue, green, yellow, and black (SEE SOURCES, PAGE 201)

4 crème wafer cookies (each 2½ inches long), chocolate flavor

½ (12-ounce) bag chocolate melting wafers (SEE SOURCES, PAGE 201)

1 Oreo cookie (have extras on hand in case it breaks)

3 packages Sour Punch Straws, green apple flavor

2 boxes Nerds, Wild Cherry/ Watermelon flavors

2 boxes Nerds, Amped Apple/ Lightning Lemon flavors

2 boxes Nerds, Strawberry/Grape flavors

① prepare the cake

Remove the frosting decorations from the cake, and trim the cake board (see pages 14 and 15). Put the cake, on its trimmed board, on a 13 × 19-inch cake board and attach with glue.

In a medium bowl, stir 2¼ cups vanilla frosting until smooth. Using an offset spatula, frost the cake. Dip the spatula in hot water, shake off the excess, and carefully smooth the frosting. Position the cake vertically on your work surface. Measure 9 inches from the bottom of the cake, and score a line across, creating a horizon line. Clean up the board and refrigerate the cake.

② shape the windmill body

Trim the top of the family-size pound cake to make it flat. Lay the cake vertically in front of you. Refer to the diagram when making the next cuts and moving the cut pieces. On the top edge, measure ¾ inch from the top left corner and make a mark. Measure ¾ inch from the top right corner and make a mark. Line up a knife between the top left mark and the bottom left corner, and cut through the cake. Repeat on the right side.

Put the cut-off pieces back in their original position, and then move the piece on the right to the left side of the cake, turning it upside down so that the rounded edge is at the bottom, crust side out (diagram 1). Repeat with the other cut-off piece. The bottom of the cake will be wider than the top and the shape will resemble a windmill body (diagram 2). Attach the pieces with a little frosting. Measure 1¼ inches from the top

end of the cake, and cut away and discard the small piece. Put the cake on a 10-inch cardboard cake circle and set it aside.

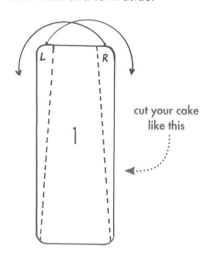

cut your cake like this

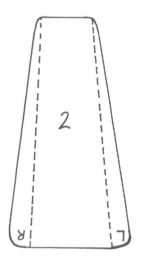

③ shape the windmill top

Put the smaller pound cake horizontally on your work surface; do not trim off any crust. Trim equal amounts off each end so the cake is 7 inches long. Cut the cake into 2 pieces: one 3 inches long and one 4 inches long. Set the 3-inch piece aside. Put the 4-inch piece horizontally and trim ½ inch off one long side so that it now measures 4 inches by 2½ inches; discard the trimmings. On the top long edge of the cake, measure

1 inch in from both the left and the right side and make a mark. Line up a knife from the left mark to the bottom left corner of the cake and cut through. Repeat on the right side; discard the trimmings. Put the cake on a plate.

4 shape the windmill base

Take the 3-inch piece of cake and flip it on its side. Trim away the top until the piece is 1 inch thick. Lay it back down and cut the length of the cake in half, creating 2 pieces that are 3 inches by 1½ inches; discard one of them and put the other on a plate.

5 frost and decorate the windmill

In a medium bowl, stir the chocolate frosting with ½ cup vanilla frosting until smooth. Using an offset spatula, frost the base piece and the angled top piece of the windmill. Clean up the plates and refrigerate the pieces.

For the large middle section of the windmill, frost the body piece of cake brown. Break up the Shredded Wheat biscuits in a bowl, and use your hands and an offset spatula to cover the center piece with the crumbled biscuits, leaving the top and bottom sides uncovered; set aside.

6 decorate the sheet cake

In a bowl, tint ¼ cup of the vanilla frosting sky blue with blue food coloring. In a separate bowl, tint ½ cup of the vanilla frosting grass green, using a 2-to-1 ratio of green and yellow food coloring.

Working as quickly as possible, use the 1-inch flat-head paintbrush to apply the green frosting to the bottom 9-inch portion of the sheet cake, completely covering the top and sides. If the cake becomes too warm, refrigerate it again and then continue. For the sky, clean and dry the paintbrush, and loosely brush blue frosting over the upper section of the cake, leaving some exposed areas white. Dip an offset spatula in hot water, shake off the excess, and carefully smooth the sky frosting, rinse the spatula, then repeat for the grass. Refrigerate.

7 make the windmill paddles

Pull apart the chocolate crème wafer cookies to make 8 pieces. Run the edge of an offset spatula between the cream filling and the cookie to remove the filling, leaving a clean cookie. Using wire cutters, cut 4 wooden skewers to 6¼-inch lengths, discarding the sharp ends.

In a microwave-safe bowl, melt the chocolate wafers at 10-second intervals, stirring until smooth. Holding one end of a skewer, completely coat it with the melted chocolate using the ½-inch flat-head paintbrush, leaving the tip where you are holding it exposed. Repeat with the remaining skewers. Set aside on a large piece of wax paper to harden.

Working on wax paper, assemble the windmill paddles: Put 2 wafer cookies end-to-end, top side down, and using the ½-inch flat-head paintbrush, coat the backs with melted chocolate. Take a chocolate-covered skewer and add a little more chocolate on one side. Push this side of the skewer lengthwise against a wafer, aligning it flush with the top of the wafer. The skewer will be longer than the wafer. Brush more chocolate to bind the pieces together, and apply chocolate liberally to fill in any cracks. Repeat for the remaining 3 paddles, making sure all wafer blades are on the same side of each skewer. If the melted chocolate becomes too thick in the bowl, microwave again. Be careful not to move the blades until they are set.

Split the Oreo cookie in half; scrape out and discard the filling. Put the cookie, textured side down, on a piece of wax paper and spread melted chocolate over it, using chocolate that is almost set rather than freshly melted. Arrange the paddles around the cookie so that the skewers are touching at the center.

Cover the center of the Oreo with enough melted chocolate to cover the surface of the cookie and the skewers. Gently press the other half of the Oreo, textured side down, on the chocolate; the paddle blades should lift parallel to the table. As the blades lift, rotate them down until they touch the table and are holding themselves up. Keep pressing on the Oreo until set (the set time will vary, depending on your environment). Wipe off any excess chocolate with your finger. Once set, put the piece aside.

8 finish the windmill body

Position the sheet cake with the sky on top. Put the base piece of the windmill on the cake, 2 inches from

CONTINUES ➡

the bottom edge. Use an offset spatula to put the body on the base, and then add the top of the windmill.

Mix ¼ cup vanilla frosting with enough black food coloring to create a charcoal gray color, and scoop it into a zip-top plastic bag. Cut ¼ inch off the tip, and pipe a border around only the top and bottom pieces of the windmill. Using a skewer and an offset spatula, clear a shallow line across the Shredded Wheat 1½ inches from the bottom of the middle section, exposing the frosting. Pipe frosting over the line. Scrape away a small section of Shredded Wheat just above the line to make the doorway. Pipe a door in the space and fill it in.

Scoop ¼ cup vanilla frosting into a plastic bag and cut ⅛ inch off the tip. Pipe two square windows on the windmill base, and pipe an outline around the door. Take the bag of charcoal frosting and pipe the window frames.

9 finish the flowerbeds and sky

Line up the Sour Punch Straws as shown in the photo, framing the grass area, and marking the separations of different colored flowerbeds. For the flowerbeds, pour the Nerds into each section, one color to a section. Clean up any stray Nerds. Lightly sprinkle green Nerds over each flowerbed.

For the sky, add ¼ cup vanilla frosting to the remaining vanilla, and cut another ⅛ inch off the tip of the bag. Squeeze out clouds.

10 assemble the windmill

On the windmill paddles, fill a zip-top plastic bag with ¼ cup vanilla frosting and cut ⅛ inch off the tip. Pipe a thin border of white frosting around the edges of the cookie wafer paddles. Pipe on a crisscross pattern. Using the charcoal frosting, pipe a line over the exposed wooden skewer.

Push a drinking straw through the center of the top section of the windmill to the bottom of the cake. Cut it to ¼ inch below the surface of the frosting. Gently put the Oreo cookie, with the windmill paddles, on top of the straw (the straw provides support for the windmill paddles). Squeeze a dollop of charcoal frosting on the center of the Oreo and pipe small white dots around it. Create a border around the base of the cake by lining up Sour Punch Straws and cutting them to fit.

chinese lantern

The beautiful hanging red lanterns found throughout China are symbols of luck and prosperity, and represent new beginnings and reunion. They are widely used during festivals like Chinese New Year and at birthday parties and weddings. This Chinese lantern cake is constructed with a small number of ingredients and is easy to create. The character on the cake means "Double Happiness."

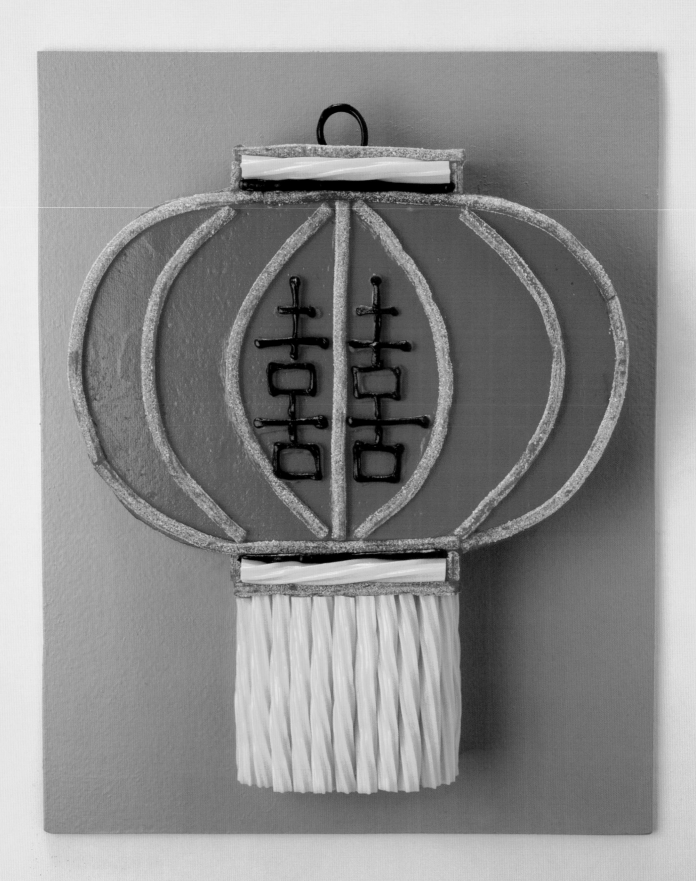

SERVES 15 TO 20
LEVEL OF DIFFICULTY: 1.5

special tools

- 1 (13 × 15-inch) cake board
- Small offset spatula

ingredients

- 2 (16-ounce) frozen pound cakes (we use Sara Lee family-size), thawed
- 3 cups vanilla frosting (2 16-ounce cans)
- Paste or gel paste food coloring: red, yellow, and black (SEE SOURCES, PAGE 201)
- 1 (10.75-ounce) frozen pound cake (we use Sara Lee), thawed
- 2 (2-ounce) packages Sour Punch Straws, strawberry flavor
- 10 yellow Twizzlers Rainbow Twists (from 2 12.4-ounce packages)
- 1 Haribo Wheel, black licorice flavor

1 shape and frost the cake

Lightly trim the tops of the family-size pound cakes to make them flat. Lay the pound cakes vertically on your work surface. Cut a ¾-inch-wide strip off the right side of each pound cake, and discard one of the strips. Cut the remaining strip to 8 inches by trimming even amounts off each end; discard the trimmings. Cut the strip in half to make two 4-inch-long strips. Position the 2 large cake pieces horizontally with the cut sides together. Measure ¾ inch diagonally from each corner and cut off and discard the corners. Put one of the 4-inch strips at the top of the cake and the other at the bottom.

In a bowl, tint 1½ cups vanilla frosting red, and scoop ¼ cup into a separate bowl for crumb-coating. Use frosting to attach the cake pieces together and the cake to the center of a 13 × 15-inch cake board, placing it 1½ inches from the top. Using an offset spatula, crumb-coat the cake. Clean up the board and refrigerate the cake.

Take the smaller pound cake (do not trim off the top or crusts) and cut equal amounts from each end to make a 3-inch-long piece. Flip the cake on its side and cut ¾ inch off the bottom, leaving intact the rounded top crust; discard all the trimmings. Put the cake on a plate, rounded top up.

In a bowl, tint ½ cup vanilla frosting yellow. Scoop 2 tablespoons into a separate bowl and crumb-coat the cake. Clean up the plate and refrigerate the cake until the frosting is firm, about 15 minutes.

Frost the larger cake with the red frosting. Spoon 2 tablespoons of the remaining red frosting into a zip-top plastic bag and set it aside. (Make more frosting if necessary.) Dip the spatula in hot water, shake off the excess, and carefully smooth the frosting. Clean up the board and refrigerate until firm, 20 to 25 minutes.

Frost the smaller cake yellow, and smooth the frosting. Refrigerate until firm, about 15 minutes.

Using your hand and an offset spatula, center the yellow cake vertically below the lantern with the top curve going from left to right.

2 decorate the lantern

Outline all the edges of the red lantern, including where it touches the board, with red Sour Punch Straws and cut to fit. Put 1 red Sour Punch Straw down the middle and 2 on either side, following the curve of the lantern. Cut to fit.

Using scissors, cut 8 yellow Twizzlers into sixteen 3½-inch-long pieces. Starting at the right edge of the yellow cake where it meets the board, line up the yellow pieces across the cake. Cut 2 yellow Twizzlers to fit across the top and bottom boxes on the lantern.

In a bowl, tint ¼ cup vanilla frosting black. Spoon it into a zip-top plastic bag and cut ⅛ inch off the tip. Pipe 1 line on the bottom of the top box and another on the top of the bottom box. Cut ⅛ inch off the tip of the reserved bag of red frosting. Following the photograph, pipe the Double Happiness symbol in red frosting first, and then pipe over it with the black frosting.

To finish the cake, cut a 3-inch piece off the black licorice wheel. Form it into a loop by firmly pinching the ends together, and put it at the center of the top box.

geek
-o-
rama

robot

You don't have to be mad or a scientist to create this colorful robot cake. All it takes is a little imagination and a handful of candies to get in touch with your inner geek. The robot has been one of our favorite cakes since we started working on the book—he seems to have a great personality! Note that if you are working in a warm climate, it's helpful to chill all the Ding Dongs, doughnuts, and Donettes in the refrigerator before starting.

SERVES 20 TO 25

LEVEL OF DIFFICULTY: 2

special tools

Small offset spatula

2 (10-inch) cardboard cake circles

2 (14-inch) cardboard cake circles

1 (19 × 26-inch) cake board covered in grease-resistant paper

1 (10-inch) wooden skewer

4 round toothpicks

ingredients

3¾ cups vanilla frosting (2½ 16-ounce cans)

Paste or gel paste food coloring: blue and black (SEE SOURCES, PAGE 201)

1 (10.75-ounce) frozen pound cake (we use Sara Lee), thawed

2 (16-ounce) frozen pound cakes (we use Sara Lee family-size), thawed

9 Rice Krispies Treats

14 Ding Dongs

2 Donettes frosted mini doughnuts, chocolate flavor

½ cup chocolate melting wafers (SEE SOURCES, PAGE 201)

2 (2-ounce) packages Sour Punch Straws, green apple flavor

3 Trolli Sour Apple-O's

3 large gumdrops: 1 yellow and 2 red

1 (3-inch) rainbow swirl lollipop

1 marshmallow

2 (3- to 3½-inch) mini Unicorn Pops

2 Oreo cookies

1 Air Heads Xtreme Sour Belt, lemonade flavor

1 Fruit by the Foot, strawberry flavor

1 Haribo Wheel, black licorice flavor

1 small box Dots

1 roll Necco Wafers, original flavor

1 small package Razzles

1 small box jujubes

1 small pack Starburst candy, original flavor

1 strip Necco Candy Buttons

1 package Giant Chewy SweeTarts

2 chocolate-covered cake doughnuts

1 make the head

In a bowl, tint the vanilla frosting bright blue using blue food coloring. Scoop 1 cup into a separate bowl for crumb-coating.

Lightly trim the top of the smaller pound cake to make it flat, and trim the sides to remove the crusts. Cut off even amounts on each side to make a 6-inch-long loaf.

Attach the cake to a 10-inch cardboard circle with some frosting. Using a knife or scissors, trim off all the excess cardboard. Put the cake, with its cut cardboard, onto a new 10-inch cardboard circle. Crumb-coat the cake with a thin layer of frosting. Clean up the cake circle and refrigerate the cake.

2 make the body

Trim the tops and sides of the 2 family-size pound cakes. Trim equal amounts off both ends to make two 9-inch-long cakes. Put the pieces together horizontally, one in front of the other, on your work surface. On the top edge, make marks ¼ inch from each side. On the bottom edge, make marks 1½ inches from each side (the top should be 8½ inches and the bottom 6 inches). Line up the two left markings and cut through. Repeat on the right side. Discard the trimmings.

Using an offset spatula, attach the pound cake pieces to each other and then to a 14-inch cake circle with frosting. Trim the excess cardboard around the cake. Put the cake, with its cut cardboard, onto a new 14-inch cardboard cake circle. Crumb-coat the cake and refrigerate until the frosting is firm, 15 to 20 minutes.

3 make the feet

Cut 1 Rice Krispies Treat in half lengthwise. Stack up 3 cereal treats, each one on its widest surface. Turn another treat on its side lengthwise, and position it against the bottom right side of the stack, touching at its widest surface. Add a half piece on top so the left and right sides are even and form a cube. Gently but firmly press the cereal treats together, using your palms to help shape and bind the cube. The cube will be about 2½ inches. Repeat for the other foot. Adhere each foot to a different plate with some frosting, and coat with blue frosting. Refrigerate until firm, 15 to 20 minutes.

4 frost the head, body, and feet

Using the blue frosting and an offset spatula, frost the head. Dip the spatula in hot water, shake off the excess, and carefully smooth the frosting. Clean up the cake circle and refrigerate the head for at least 30 minutes, until firm. In the meantime, frost the body in the same manner and refrigerate until firm, about 30 minutes. Frost the feet a second time. Smooth the frosting and refrigerate.

5 assemble the robot

Keeping the cut cardboard piece attached for support, use your hand and an offset spatula to lift the head onto your paper-lined cake board, centering it 6 inches from the top of the board. Put 1 Ding Dong on its side, with the bottom against the head, to form the neck. If the Ding Dong is higher than the head, trim the underside until it is flush. Repeat with a second Ding Dong on top of the head.

With the cut cardboard piece still attached, put the body on the board with the wide side against the neck. Center 1 Donette on each side of the head, bottom side against the cake.

In a microwave-safe bowl, melt the chocolate wafers at 10-second intervals, stirring until smooth. Spoon the chocolate into a zip-top plastic bag and cut ⅛ inch off the tip with scissors.

6 make the arms

Put 1 Ding Dong on its side ¼ inch below the shoulder, bottom side against the cake. If necessary, trim the underside of the Ding Dong to match the height of the body. Stagger the second and third Ding Dongs downward, bottom-to-top, placing each one ¼ inch below the previous one, and attach the segments with melted chocolate. Repeat for the other arm.

7 make the legs

The robot's legs are assembled independently and placed on the body later. Put 3 Ding Dongs on their sides and trim the undersides to the height of the body cake. Attach the Ding Dongs to each other, bottom-to-top, with the melted chocolate. Repeat for the other leg.

Pipe a line of chocolate over each Ding Dong seam, and wrap a green Sour Punch Straw around it, cutting to fit and tucking the ends under. Press lightly to adhere them. Repeat for the arms. Wrap a green Sour Punch Straw around the top of the neck and around the Ding Dong on the head, as well as around the ears. Using melted chocolate, attach 1 gummy Apple-O to the center of each Donette ear, white side down.

Slide an offset spatula under the legs and place them, centered, below the body. Attach the feet to the legs.

8 decorate the robot's head

Use the flat end of a skewer to drill through 1 large yellow gumdrop. Using melted chocolate, attach the gumdrop to the top of the Ding Dong at the head. Push the rainbow swirl lollipop through the gumdrop hole and through the Ding Dong until only ¾ inch of the stick is exposed. Put a marshmallow under the lollipop head to level it. Insert one of the mini Unicorn Pops into each Apple-O ear.

For the eyes, carefully open 2 Oreo cookies to keep the icing on one cookie, and discard the cookies without the icing. Scrape any crumbs off the icing, using a small offset spatula, or cover the crumbs with a small amount of vanilla frosting. Put the Oreo cookie eyes on the face against the top edge of the head. Cut the thickness of 2 large red gumdrops in half and put the rounded parts on the Oreo eyes, with one along the top and the other along the bottom, as shown.

For the mouth, cut a 5-inch piece of the lemonade Xtreme Sour Belt and center it ½ inch above the bottom of the head. In a bowl, tint 2 tablespoons vanilla frosting black. Spoon the frosting into a zip-top plastic bag and cut ⅛ inch off the tip. Pipe a wavy line for the mouth within the yellow area.

9 make the belt

Cut a 12-inch piece of strawberry Fruit by the Foot. Put the belt 1½ inches from the bottom of the body, draping it over the body and down both sides to the cake board, cutting to fit.

Spoon the remaining blue frosting into a zip-top plastic bag and cut ⅛ inch off the tip. Pipe frosting on the back of a black licorice wheel and attach it to the center of the belt. Then attach an Apple-O, green side up, and 1 orange Dot to the center of the ring. Attach 2 Necco Wafers on each side of the belt, and 1 Razzle to the top of each.

CONTINUES ➡

10 decorate the robot's body

Put 11 jujubes, evenly spaced, along the bottom edge. Line up 4 Starburst candies on the top right corner, and put 1 Necco Candy Button on each Starburst. Put 4 Dots in a diamond shape on the top left corner, and center 2 Dots under the row of Starbursts. On the top of each shoulder, attach 3 jujubes. Attach 1 Giant Chewy SweeTart to the top of each foot, and attach 1 Necco Wafer on top of each SweeTart.

11 add the frosting details

Using the blue frosting, pipe 1 large dot on each corner of the head and a line of smaller dots around the face. Do the same around the feet. On the torso, pipe a rectangle of small dots around the Starbursts, with large dots at the corners. Pipe a diamond around the Dots in the same manner. At the belt, pipe a large dot above and below the licorice wheel, and lines of smaller dots in between.

12 make the hands

Cut a 2-inch-long wedge from each cake doughnut and discard the trimmings. Re-melt the chocolate in the plastic bag, and use it to attach the doughnut hands to the arms, as shown. Secure the hands by inserting 2 toothpicks through each doughnut to the arms. Attach 2 brown Necco Wafers to the cut ends of the doughnuts with black frosting, and pipe 4 black lines on each.

motherboard

In computers, the motherboard—also known as a mainboard or logic board—is a printed circuit board that connects the essential components together. It holds the central processing unit (CPU), the memory, and the peripherals, and is the heart of the computer. Any computer geek will go crazy for this cake, with its intricate "wiring" and realistic design that may very well fool him or her.

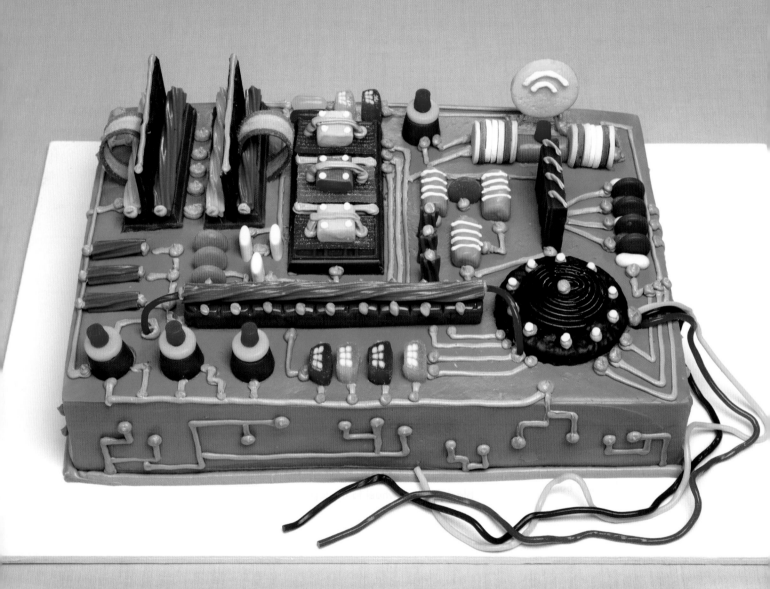

SERVES 20 TO 25
LEVEL OF DIFFICULTY: 1.5

special tools

1 (12 × 18-inch) cake board

Small offset spatula

4 round toothpicks

ingredients

1 (8 × 12-inch) sheet cake (¼ sheet) with vanilla frosting

3 cups vanilla frosting (2 16-ounce cans)

Paste or gel paste food coloring: green and black (SEE SOURCES, PAGE 201)

½ cup chocolate melting wafers (SEE SOURCES, PAGE 201)

1 Haribo Wheel, black licorice flavor

1 (1.4-ounce) York Peppermint Pattie

1 large (2.25-ounce) Tootsie Roll (6 inches long)

5 Twizzlers Rainbow Twists: 3 blue and 2 yellow

12 Spree candies: 4 yellow, 1 red, 4 purple, and 3 orange

4 Rolo candies

5 red jujubes

1 (1.5-ounce) KitKat bar

1 (1.45-ounce) Hershey's Special Dark chocolate bar

1 Hershey's milk chocolate bar, king-size

3 Rips Bite-Size Licorice Pieces: 2 red and 1 green

3 Starburst candies: 2 yellow and 1 red

14 Necco wafers

4 Tootsie Fruit Rolls: 1 red and 3 orange

1 yellow Giant Chewy SweeTart

2 Mike and Ike candies, Original Fruits flavor: 1 yellow and 1 red

6 Haribo Brixx candies: 3 yellow and 3 red

5 Good & Plenty candies: 3 white and 2 red

3 pieces Trident White gum

2 pieces Air Heads Xtremes Sweetly Sour Belts, Rainbow Berry flavor

4 Rips Whips licorice laces: 2 red, 1 yellow, and 1 blue

1 prepare the cake

Remove the frosting decorations from the sheet cake and trim the cake board (see pages 14 and 15). Put the cake, on its trimmed board, on a 12 × 18-inch cake board and attach with glue.

In a bowl, tint 1½ cups vanilla frosting green. Using an offset spatula, frost the cake. Dip the spatula in hot water, shake off the excess, and carefully smooth the frosting. Clean up the cake board.

2 assemble the circuitry

In a microwave-safe bowl, melt the chocolate wafers at 10-second intervals, stirring until the chocolate is smooth. Spoon the chocolate into a zip-top plastic bag and cut ⅛ inch off the tip. Use the chocolate to attach the black licorice wheel to the top of the Peppermint Pattie, and put it on the cake, 1 inch from the right edge and ¾ inch from the bottom edge.

Take the Tootsie Roll, and use the edge of an offset spatula to make the indentations in it deeper. Cut 1 blue Twizzler the same length as the Tootsie Roll and attach it to the top with melted chocolate. Center the Tootsie Roll on the cake, placing it ¼ inch to the left of the Peppermint Pattie.

Attach 4 yellow Sprees to the tops of 4 Rolos with melted chocolate, and attach 4 red

jujubes to the tops of the Sprees. Starting ½ inch from the left edge of the cake and from the bottom, place 3 Rolos ½ inch apart. Set aside the fourth Rolo.

Break the KitKat bar in half lengthwise, making 2 groups of 2 wafers. Split the Hershey's Special Dark chocolate bar into 4 pieces of 3 segments each. In the crevice of each of the 2 KitKat bar halves, stand up 5 chocolate segments (a group of 3 and a group of 2). If the chocolate segments won't stand up, pipe some melted chocolate to attach them. Cut 2 yellow and 2 blue Twizzlers the same length as the KitKat halves, and attach 1 yellow and 1 blue Twizzler to each side of the KitKat, as shown in the photo. Put 1 KitKat on the cake, placing it ¾ inch from the left edge and ⅛ inch from the top, and put the second KitKat ¼ inch to the right of the first.

Break off 1 of the 4 sections from the Hershey's king-size milk chocolate bar and set it aside. Take the larger piece, and attach 2 red Rips Bite-Size pieces on

CONTINUES ➡

the top and bottom sections and 1 green Rips piece in the middle. On top of the Rips, attach 2 yellow and 1 red Starburst candy, as shown. Put this piece on the cake, 1 inch from the top edge and centered above the Tootsie Roll.

Create 2 stacks of 7 Necco wafers each, attaching them with melted chocolate in between. Lay 1 stack on its side on the cake, 1½ inches from the top and 1 inch from the right edge. Put 1 red Tootsie Fruit Roll lengthwise in the center to the left of the stack, and attach 1 red jujube to the top. Put the second stack of wafers on its side against the left side of the Tootsie Fruit Roll.

Insert 2 toothpicks ¼ inch into the bottom of a yellow Giant SweeTart, spacing them ½ inch apart at a 45-degree angle. Insert the yellow SweeTart ½ inch from the top edge of the cake, lining it up with the center of the red jujube on the Tootsie Fruit Roll. Leave ½ inch of the toothpicks exposed,

and smooth over any marks on the frosting with an offset spatula dipped in hot water.

Take the reserved small section of the Hershey's milk chocolate bar and insert 2 toothpicks on the broken side. Put it on the cake, centered between the Peppermint Pattie and the Necco Wafer stacks.

Starting at the top of the cake, above the Starbursts, put 1 yellow and 1 red Mike and Ike horizontally, and 1 yellow and 1 red Brixx vertically. To the right, put the reserved Rolo. Below the Rolo, arrange 3 orange Tootsie Fruit Rolls vertically, forming a triangle, and insert 1 red Spree between the top 2 pieces. Cut three 1-inch lengths of blue Twizzlers and insert them vertically to the left of the bottom orange Tootsie Fruit Roll.

On the right side of the cake, parallel to the chocolate bar, arrange 1 white Good & Plenty, 1 purple Spree, 1 red Good & Plenty, and repeat, ending with a white Good & Plenty. At the bottom of the cake, put 2 red and 2 yellow Brixx in an alternating pattern. On the left side of the cake between the KitKats and the Tootsie Roll, place three 1-inch pieces of blue Twizzlers horizontally. Insert 3 orange Sprees in a vertical line above the left end of the Tootsie Roll, and arrange 3 Trident White gum pieces in a triangle to the right of the orange Spree.

3 pipe the details

In a bowl, tint 1 cup vanilla frosting gray using black food coloring. Divide the frosting into 2 zip-top plastic bags and cut ⅛ inch off the tips. On the Peppermint Pattie, pipe 10 gray dots around the licorice wheel and 1 dot in the center. On

top of the standing Hershey's milk chocolate section, pipe 4 diagonal lines. Pipe 1 dot on each of the 3 standing blue Twizzler pieces. On the large Tootsie Roll, pipe 1 dot in each segment on both sides of the blue Twizzler. Pipe a small gray dot on both ends of the blue Twizzler opening. Pipe 1 line with 2 dots at the ends across each of the 3 Starbursts, and a line on the seams between the Rips pieces.

On top of both Hershey's Special Dark chocolate bar pieces standing in the KitKats, pipe a line down the full length of the chocolate. Pipe 1 dot on both ends of the blue and yellow Twizzlers. Pipe 1 dot on each end of the 3 blue horizontal Twizzlers pieces.

Use the photo as a guide for connecting all the circuitry. Pipe the lines from section to section, piping a dot where a line connects

with an object and where the line ends. On the sides of the cake, pipe connecting lines sparsely. Pipe a gray border around the base of the cake.

In a small bowl, stir ¼ cup vanilla frosting until smooth. Spoon it into a zip-top plastic bag and cut ⅛ inch off the tip. On top of the gray dots on the Peppermint Pattie, pipe a small white dot. Pipe 4 lines across the orange Fruit Rolls, 4 small dots on the corners of each of the Starbursts, and 2 curved white lines on the Giant SweeTart.

④ make the wires

Cut two 3-inch strips from the Rainbow Sour Belt. In a microwave, melt the chocolate in the plastic bag in 5- to 10-second intervals until smooth. In the crevice between

the KitKat and the yellow Twizzler, pipe a line of chocolate the width of the belt; shape the belt into a loop around the yellow Twizzler, and attach it underneath, gently pushing it into the cake. Repeat on the opposite side.

Cut 1 of the red Rips Whips into two 3-inch-long pieces and insert 1 piece into each end of the long blue Twizzler, pushing the other ends into the cake. Pipe a small gray dot where the wires enter the cake.

Take 1 full-length red Rips Whips, gently push one end under the Peppermint Pattie, and carefully drape it off the side, laying it on the board in front of the cake. Repeat with 1 yellow and 1 blue Rips Whips. Finish by piping 1 gray dot where the wires meet at the Peppermint Pattie.

turntable

My favorite part of this edible turntable is the tone arm. The first time Rick made this cake, I could barely resist moving it to play the record! It's a fairly complicated part of the cake, and it took a bit of experimenting on Rick's part to discover the perfect way to create the tone arm: inserting a wire into a licorice straw, then into a marshmallow to suspend it. Brilliant!

SERVES 20 TO 25
LEVEL OF DIFFICULTY: 2

special tools

- 1 (9 × 13-inch) cake board
  Small offset spatula
- 2 (6-inch) cardboard cake circles
- 1 (8-inch) cardboard cake circle
- 1 (10-inch) wooden skewer
  ½-inch flat-head paintbrush
  Wire cutters
- 1 (18- to 22-gauge) cloth- or
  paper-covered wire, 7 inches long

ingredients

- 1 (8 × 12-inch) sheet cake (¼ sheet)
  with vanilla frosting
- 3 cups vanilla frosting
  (2 16-ounce cans)
  Paste or gel paste food coloring:
  black (SEE SOURCES, PAGE 201)
- 1 (10.75-ounce) frozen pound cake
  (we use Sara Lee), thawed
- 5 black Twizzlers
- 2 Giant Chewy SweeTarts, any color
- 1 Air Heads Xtremes Sweetly Sour
  Belt, Rainbow Berry flavor
- 5 jujubes: 4 red and 1 purple
- 1 (7.8-ounce) box Jujyfruits (only
  black is used)
- 1 Haribo Wheel, black licorice flavor
- 1 Sour Punch Straw, any flavor
- 1 marshmallow

1 prepare the cake

Remove the frosting decorations from the sheet cake, preserving the squared edges, and trim the cake board (see pages 14 and 15). Put the cake, on its trimmed board, on a 9 × 13-inch cake board and attach with glue.

In a bowl, tint 1½ cups vanilla frosting gray using black food coloring. Using an offset spatula, frost the cake. Dip the spatula in hot water, shake off the excess, and carefully smooth the frosting. Clean up the board and refrigerate the cake.

2 make the disc

Lightly trim the top of the pound cake to make it flat, and lightly remove the crusts. Cut the thickness of the cake in half and put the halves together horizontally side by side. Use a 6-inch cardboard cake circle as a stencil to cut the pound cake into a disc. Discard the trimmings.

In a bowl, tint ⅓ cup vanilla frosting black. Put the trimmed cake pieces on a 6-inch cardboard circle and attach the pieces to each other and to the cake circle with black frosting. Put the cake, on its cake circle, onto an 8-inch cardboard cake circle. Frost the disc with a thin layer of frosting, and smooth. Clean up the cake circle and refrigerate the cake until the frosting is firm, 20 to 25 minutes.

Take the sheet cake and center a 6-inch cardboard cake circle on top of it, 1 inch from the left edge. Score a line around the circle with a skewer, and then lift it off the cake. Using an offset spatula, put the disc cake, with its 6-inch cardboard cake circle

attached, onto the marked circle. With the skewer, score a vertical line 1 inch to the right of the disc cake to divide the turntable from the control panel.

3 add the details

Trim the tapered ends off 3 black Twizzlers and wrap the Twizzlers around the base of the disc cake. Put two 1½-inch-long pieces of black Twizzlers at each corner of the base of the sheet cake. In a bowl, tint ⅓ cup vanilla frosting a light gray with black food coloring. Fill a zip-top plastic bag with the frosting and cut ¼ inch off the tip. Pipe a border around the top edge of the cake, a line on each side of the bottom connecting the Twizzlers, and a line over the scored dividing line.

4 make the control panel

Use a ½-inch flat-head paintbrush to brush black frosting over the top and sides of 2 Giant SweeTarts. Put them on the lower right corner of the cake. Cut a 3-inch-long piece of Air Heads Xtremes Sweetly Sour Belt. Put it 1 inch from the top and ¼ inch to the right of the dividing line. Using the gray frosting, pipe a border around the belt. Pipe a box for the mixer, placing it ½ inch to the right with the same height and twice the width of the belt. Pipe 3 evenly spaced gray lines inside the box.

In a bowl, tint ⅓ cup vanilla frosting black. Fill a zip-top plastic bag with the frosting and cut ⅛ inch off the tip. Pipe a black line over the gray border around the Sour Belt and mixer boxes and on the lines inside the mixer box. Pipe a 1½-inch-long horizontal line 1 inch below the belt.

Put the 5 jujubes at the top edge of the cake. Put 1 round black Jujyfruit on top of each Giant SweeTart knob, and 2 to the right of the black horizontal line in the control panel. Put 1 oval black Jujyfruit vertically over the horizontal black line. Put 2 round black Jujyfruits centered on the lower left corner of the cake. Cut 2 more oval Jujyfruits in half and put 3 halves on the lines in the mixer box. On the top center of the disc, put a black licorice wheel.

5 make the tone arm

Cut a 5-inch piece off a Sour Punch Straw. Insert the 7-inch wire into the Sour Punch Straw with 1 inch exposed on each end. Bend the wire 45 degrees on one end. Using the ½-inch flat-head paintbrush, brush a thin layer of black frosting over the Straw. Coat a marshmallow with a thin layer of black frosting, and insert the straight end of the wire into it. Insert an oval black Jujyfruit onto the bent wire at the other end. Put the tone arm on the cake to the left of the control panel. Put 1 black round Jujyfruit under the head for support, and attach it with gray frosting.

6 finish the cake

Spoon the remaining gray frosting into a zip-top plastic bag and cut ⅛ inch off the tip. (Make an additional ¼ cup, if necessary.) Referring to the photo, pipe all the gray line and dot details. Finish by piping the small black dots on top of some of the gray dots.

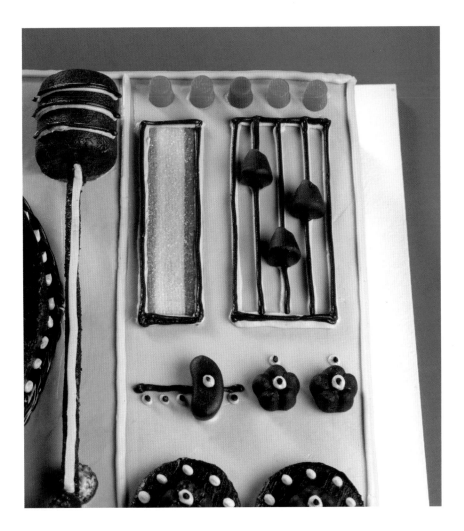

ray gun

Be ready to take on an alien army with this high-powered retro ray gun cake. Rick's had an interest in science fiction since childhood, and his clever design will resonate with any sci-fi fan. When the cake is done, you can imagine the sounds and the beams of energy blasting from the tip. Galactic invaders beware!

SERVES 5 TO 8
LEVEL OF DIFFICULTY: 3

special tools

- 1 (13 × 19-inch) cake board
- **Small offset spatula**

ingredients

- 1 **(16-ounce) frozen pound cake (we use Sara Lee family-size), thawed**
- 1 **(10.75-ounce) frozen pound cake (we use Sara Lee), thawed**
- 3 **cups vanilla frosting (2 16-ounce cans)**
- **Paste or gel paste food coloring: blue, black, red, and yellow**
  (SEE SOURCES, PAGE 201)
- 1 **Ding Dong**
- 1 **Haribo Wheel, strawberry flavor**
- 4 **Dots: 3 red and 1 yellow**
- 2 **pink Twizzlers, Rainbow Twists flavor**
- 6 **red Sixlets**
- 1 **(2-ounce) package Air Heads Xtremes Lemonade Sour Belts**
- 5 **Giant Chewy SweeTarts: 2 yellow and 3 red (from 3 1.5-ounce packages)**
- 1 **large red gumdrop**
- 1 **Twizzlers Pull 'n' Peel rope**

1 shape the ray gun

Put the family-size pound cake horizontally on a work surface with the rounded side up. Measure 1½ inches from the right side and score a vertical line (line A). Stand up the cake on its left short side, making sure line A is facing left. Score a vertical line down the middle of the top surface (line B), and put the cake back in its original position. Flip the cake on its side with line A facing you, line up a knife on the top surface between line A and line B, and cut through. Discard the trimming.

Flip the cake back to its original position and rotate it so the cut wedge side is facing you. On the closest top edge, make a mark ¾ inch from each side. (It should measure 2 inches between the marks.) Line up the knife with the left mark and the left end of line A, and cut through; set the corner aside. Repeat on the right side and discard the corner. Set the cake aside.

2 make the handle

Trim the top of the smaller pound cake to make it flat. Flip the cake on its side and cut its thickness in half. Set aside the top part of the cake. Put the bottom piece horizontally on a work surface. On the top edge of the cake, measure 3½ inches from the right side and make a mark. On the bottom edge, measure 2½ inches from the right side and make a mark. Line up a knife between the two marks and cut away the piece at an angle, discarding the smaller piece.

3 make the ray gun tip

Take the reserved top half of the pound cake and cut equal amounts off both ends to make it 4 inches long. Reduce its width to 2 inches. Discard all trimmings. Position the cake vertically. On the top edge closest to you, make a mark in the center. Line up a knife between the mark and the top left corner on the same surface and cut through. Repeat on the right side to create a triangle. Discard the trimmings.

Orient the triangle horizontally and cut its length in half, discarding the pointed piece. Put the wide side of the remaining piece against the small end of the ray gun body. Make any adjustments so that they align before attaching.

4 assemble the ray gun

In a bowl, tint 1½ cups vanilla frosting a bright blue using blue and a touch of black food coloring mixed together. Scoop ⅓ cup into a separate bowl for crumb-coating.

Put the body of the ray gun on a 13 × 19-inch cake board, 1½ inches from the left side and 3 inches from the top. Position the handle underneath to the left, with the angled side against the body. Take the reserved corner piece and put the cut side against the body to the right of the handle to make the trigger.

Put the tip of the ray gun against the body. Cut 1 Ding Dong in half and put it on top of the body, flush with the left side, forming the rounded top piece.

Using the crumb-coat frosting, attach all the cake pieces together, and attach the cake to the cake board. Crumb-coat the cake. Clean up the board and refrigerate the cake until the frosting is firm, 20 to 25 minutes.

Using an offset spatula, frost the cake blue, maintaining the definition of the pieces. Dip the spatula in hot water, shake off the excess, and carefully smooth the frosting. Clean up the board and refrigerate until firm, 20 to 25 minutes.

⑤ decorate the ray gun

Put ¼ cup vanilla frosting into each of three bowls. Tint one bowl gray with black food coloring, tint the second red, and tint the third yellow. Fill 3 zip-top plastic bags with the three frostings, and fill 1 more bag with the leftover blue used to frost the ray gun.

Cut ¼ inch off the tip of the red frosting bag. Following the contour of the handle, pipe an outline in red, staying within ½ inch of any side. Fill it in by piping thin horizontal lines back and forth. Carefully smooth the frosting.

Cut ¼ inch off the tip of the yellow frosting bag. Pipe the outline of a dime-size dot in the middle of the handle, fill it in, and smooth the frosting. Pipe lines to resemble a yellow starburst.

Working on the left side of the ray gun, pipe one 3-inch-long yellow line following the top edge, and another following the bottom edge of the body. Join the ends together in an arc where the center point is 1½ inches wide. Fill in by piping thin yellow lines, and smooth the frosting.

Cut ¼ inch off the tip of the blue frosting bag and pipe an outline around the top edges of the handle and the top part of the trigger, including where it joins the body, and around the red area in the handle. Pipe outlines around the rest of the gun body, including the yellow section. Pipe a line that separates the body from the slope. Pipe a line across the seam where the tip meets the body. Pipe a line around the entire base of the ray gun.

Pipe a blue rectangle that is 3½ inches long by 2 inches wide on the top right side of the gun body. Cut 1 red licorice wheel in half and put one of the halves in front of the yellow section. Pipe 1 blue pea-size dot in the center of the licorice wheel and 1 red dot on top of that. Put the other licorice wheel half flush with the top of the cake above the Ding Dong.

On the rounded top piece, pipe a yellow line contoured to the licorice wheel; pipe 1 red line around that, and add a yellow dot in the middle. Pipe 3 evenly spaced red lines contoured with the curve in the yellow section. Put 2 red Dots and 1 yellow Dot under the blue rectangle. Cut ⅛ inch off the tip of the gray frosting bag and pipe 7 evenly spaced lines in the blue rectangle. Pipe 8 red dots between the lines. Below the Dots, pipe two 4-inch-long gray lines, ¼ inch apart. Pipe 5 evenly spaced yellow dots in between.

Cut five 2-inch-long pieces from the pink Rainbow Twizzlers, and put them on the slope of the gun, evenly spaced. Put 6 red Sixlets between the Twizzler pieces at the narrow end of the slope. Pipe 4 yellow dots between each pair of Twizzlers.

⑥ finish the ray gun tip

Cut a 3½-inch-long piece of the Lemonade Sour Belt and wrap it around the section where the tip meets the slope, cutting to fit. To the right of the belt, pipe 4 evenly spaced red lines around the tip. Cut ¼ inch off 2 red and 2 yellow Giant SweeTarts, and put them, cut side down, on the tip of the ray gun, alternating colors and attaching them to each other with yellow frosting. Slice ⅛ inch off the top and bottom of the giant red gumdrop and set the remaining piece against the red Giant SweeTart half. Cut a 1½-inch-long piece of the Twizzlers Pull 'n' Peel rope and put it at the end of the red gumdrop. Put the flat side of a red Dot at the end of the Twizzler.

⑦ finish the trigger

Cut 1 red Giant Chewy SweeTart in half and put one half at an angle flush against the handle. Discard the other half. Pipe a gray outline around the trigger and a small dot on the section above it.

camera

Present this picture-perfect digital camera to your favorite shutterbug or techie and prepare to say "cake" instead of "cheese." You'll see that the design is simple and has minimal decorations, so take your time frosting the cake to get as smooth a surface as possible, and practice your piping technique to get the details as precise as you can!

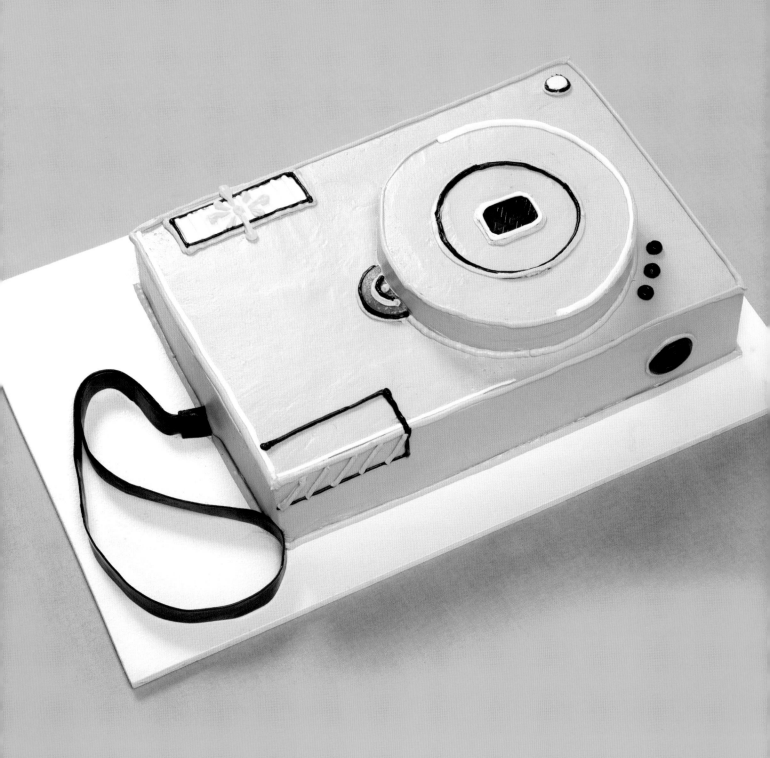

SERVES 20 TO 25
LEVEL OF DIFFICULTY: 2.5

special tools

- 1 (13 × 19-inch) cake board
  Small offset spatula
- 1 (6-inch) cardboard cake circle
- 1 (8-inch) cardboard cake circle
  ½-inch flat-head paintbrush
- 1 round toothpick

ingredients

- 1 (8 × 12-inch) sheet cake (¼ sheet) with vanilla frosting
- 3¾ cups vanilla frosting (2½ 16-ounce cans)
  Paste or gel paste food coloring: black and yellow (SEE SOURCES, PAGE 201)
- 1 (16-ounce) frozen pound cake (we use Sara Lee family-size), thawed
- 1 (2-ounce) roll Hubba Bubba Bubble Tape, Green Apple flavor
- 2 sticks Wrigley's Doublemint gum
  Pure lemon extract
  Liquid food coloring: black (SEE SOURCES, PAGE 201)
- 2 purple Giant Chewy SweeTarts (from 2 1.5-ounce packages)
- 1 large black gumdrop
- 1 purple jujube

① prepare the cake

Remove the frosting decorations from the sheet cake and trim the cake board (see pages 14 and 15). Put the cake, with its trimmed board, horizontally on a 13 × 19-inch cake board, centering it vertically 1½ inches from the right edge. Glue it down to attach.

In a bowl, tint 2½ cups vanilla frosting gray using black paste food coloring. Scoop 1 cup into a separate bowl, and scoop 2 tablespoons from that bowl into a third one for crumb-coating. Using the remaining gray frosting from the first bowl and an offset spatula, frost the sheet cake. Dip the spatula in hot water, shake off the excess, and carefully smooth the frosting. Clean up the board and refrigerate the cake.

② make the lens

Lightly trim the top of the pound cake to make it flat, and remove the side crusts. Flip the cake on its side and cut its thickness in half. Flip the halves onto their widest sides and put them together side by side. Using a 6-inch cardboard cake circle as a stencil, cut the cake around it; discard the trimmings. Attach the cake pieces to each other and to the 6-inch cardboard cake circle with a small amount of frosting. Put the cake on the 8-inch cake circle. Crumb-coat the lens. Clean up the cake circle and refrigerate.

③ make the strap and shutter

Cover your work surface with a large piece of wax paper. Cut a 27-inch-long piece of the bubblegum tape and lay it down. For the strap connector, cut the length of 1 stick of Doublemint gum in half; discard one half.

For the camera shutter, cut 1 stick of Doublemint gum into 3 pieces by first cutting the length in half and cutting one of the halves in half lengthwise. Line up 1 small and 1 large cut piece, with the longest edges together. Cut off the 4 corners, and discard the trimmings and the remaining small piece. Lay out all the cut pieces on the wax paper.

In a bowl, mix 1 teaspoon lemon extract and 1 teaspoon black liquid food coloring. Using a ½-inch flat-head paintbrush, paint the tops of all the gum pieces. When the strap dries, paint the other side. Set all the pieces aside.

④ frost and place the lens

Frost the lens cake gray, and smooth the frosting. Clean up the cake circle and refrigerate until firm, 30 minutes.

Assemble the sheet cake and the lens cake: Using your hand and an offset spatula, carefully place the lens, on its 6-inch cardboard, on the sheet cake, 1½ inches from the right and ½ inch from the bottom.

Take a frosting can lid (one that is not warped) and press the raised side of the lid onto the middle of the lens to score a mark. Remove the lid.

⑤ decorate the camera

Put the gum shutter pieces on the center of the lens cake. Cut 1 purple SweeTart in half and put it to the left of the lens on the sheet cake, with the cut side against the lens. Rotate the cake board so the top side of the camera is facing you. Pierce another purple SweeTart with a toothpick, and put it, centered, on top of the camera, 1½ inches from the right. Cut the thickness of 1 large black gumdrop in half and place the dome side on the SweeTart for the camera button. Put 1 purple jujube to the left of the button.

6 make the flash

In a small bowl, stir ¼ cup vanilla frosting until smooth. Spoon it into a zip-top plastic bag and cut ⅛ inch off the tip. With the top side of the camera still facing you, pipe a 1 × 3-inch rectangle 1 inch from the right and ¼ inch from the bottom edge. Fill in the rectangle by piping thin horizontal lines back and forth, and smooth the frosting. Pipe 10 vertical lines, ¼ inch apart, in the rectangle. On the opposite corner of the cake, pipe a dime-size white dot.

7 add the frosting details

Fill a zip-top plastic bag with ⅓ cup of the remaining gray frosting and cut ⅛ inch off the tip. Pipe a border around the base and top of the cake, around the top and base of the lens, and around the shutter. Pipe around the scored circle in the middle of the lens. Pipe curved lines around the rounded side of the half SweeTart and running through the middle, and a dot inside. Pipe a border around the small white dot in the corner.

Pipe a gray border around the flash. Pipe small, evenly spaced

lines, about ⅛ inch apart, around the side of the SweeTart camera button to resemble grooves. On the top side of the cake, centered with the camera lens, pipe a lengthwise "I" that is 2½ inches long. Using the white frosting, pipe a line down the middle of the "I."

Turn the cake around so that the camera is right side up. Working inside the gray border, pipe a white frosting "L" around the left side of the cake, a half-circle around the right side of the lens, and a border around the rectangular lens piece.

In a bowl, tint ¼ cup vanilla frosting black, and spoon it into a plastic bag. Cut ⅛ inch off the tip. Make the 3-sided compartment for the battery: Starting 1 inch above the bottom left-hand corner, pipe a 3-inch-long line parallel to the bottom edge. Turn the line 90 degrees and run it down, over the edge, and back along the bottom side of the camera. Opposite the battery compartment, pipe a quarter-size black dot where a tripod would attach. Pipe 3 pea-size dots for the microphone on the lower right side. Pipe a black line around the lens circle inside the gray line.

Pipe 2 black lines next to the gray lines on the half SweeTart, a border around the flash, and a circular border around the white dot. Pipe a black line along the top portion of the "I."

8 attach the camera strap

Make a loop with the bubblegum tape and pinch the ends together to taper the strap into a 1-inch point. Push the tapered end into the left side of the cake, where it meets the board. Wrap the remaining black bubblegum piece around the base of the strap.

Using the gray frosting, pipe a line around the strap where it meets the camera. On the battery compartment, pipe 6 diagonal lines across the bottom and a circle around the black tripod hole.

9 finish the flash

In a bowl, tint 2 tablespoons vanilla frosting yellow and spoon it into a zip-top plastic bag. Cut ⅛ inch off the tip. Pipe a yellow starburst in the middle of the flash, as shown.

summer
LUVIN'

aloha shirt

The Aloha shirt—also referred to as a Hawaiian shirt—is an iconic symbol of Hawaii and suits the relaxed tropical lifestyle of the islands. The lightweight, short-sleeved dress shirt has a floral print and a collar, and is worn on the islands as a replacement for more formal business attire. To design the Aloha shirt cake, we chose one of the things we love most about Hawaii: the beautiful Plumeria flowers, which have an intoxicating fragrance.

SERVES 25
LEVEL OF DIFFICULTY: 3

special tools

- 1 (14 × 21-inch) cake board
- **Small offset spatula**
- 1 (10-inch) wooden skewer
- **#4 round artist's paintbrush**

ingredients

- 1 (12 × 8-inch) sheet cake (¼ sheet) with vanilla frosting
- 1 (16-ounce) frozen pound cake (we use Sara Lee family-size), thawed
- 5¼ cups vanilla frosting (3½ 16-ounce cans)
- **Paste or gel paste food coloring: blue, black, and yellow** (SEE SOURCES, PAGE 201)
- 7 marshmallows
- **Cornstarch, for dusting**
- 14 sticks Wrigley's Spearmint gum
- ¾ cup finely ground vanilla wafers
- ¼ cup granulated sugar

1 prepare the cake

Remove the frosting decorations from the sheet cake and trim the cake board (see pages 14 and 15).

2 shape the shirt

Lightly trim the top of the pound cake to make it flat, and remove the side crusts. Cut equal amounts off each end to make a 6-inch-long cake; set the trimmings aside. To make the diagonal cut of the sleeves, position the pound cake horizontally. Measure 4½ inches from the right across the top of the cake, and make a mark. Measure 4½ inches from the left across the bottom and make a mark. Slice diagonally through the cake at the marks. Flip the left piece over; it will be the left sleeve.

Set the sheet cake on a work surface vertically, and put the sleeves 1 inch below the top edge with their diagonal sides against the sheet cake. Position your knife against the outer edge of a sleeve, and cut away the corner of the sheet cake to round off the shoulder; repeat on the other side. Cut away any exposed cardboard with scissors. Remove the sleeves from the cake and set them aside.

Put the sheet cake vertically, on its trimmed board, in the center of a 14 × 21-inch cake board that is oriented horizontally and attach it with glue. Position the sleeves on the cake as before. Ideally, the sleeves will be less thick than the sheet cake for a more realistic appearance. To make the collar, cut away a ½-inch-wide strip of

the rounded part of one of the pound cake trimmings, and put it at the top of the cake, rounded side up, flush with the top edge.

3 frost the cake

In a bowl, tint 3 cups vanilla frosting a medium blue using blue food coloring. Spoon 1 cup of the blue frosting into a separate bowl for crumb-coating. Using an offset spatula, crumb-coat the cake with a thin layer of frosting. Refrigerate the cake until the frosting is firm, 20 to 25 minutes.

Frost the cake blue, being careful to maintain any height variation between the trunk and the sleeves of the shirt. Dip a spatula in hot water, shake off the excess, and smooth the frosting. Clean up the board and refrigerate until firm, 30 to 40 minutes.

In a bowl, tint ½ cup vanilla frosting a light gray using black food coloring. Spoon the gray frosting into a zip-top plastic bag and cut ⅛ inch off the tip. In the center of the cake, starting 1 inch below the top edge, pipe a 3-inch-long curved gray line following the contour of the top of the collar. Measure 3 inches down from the middle of the gray line and pipe a small gray dot. Create a triangle by connecting the piped dot with the curved line. Fill in the triangle by piping thin lines back and forth, and smooth the frosting.

Pipe a gray border around the sleeve openings and the bottom opening of the shirt. Fill in the area with thin lines, and smooth the frosting.

4 add the shirt details

Using a skewer, lightly score the outline of the collar. In a bowl, tint 1 cup blue frosting a darker shade with more blue food coloring. Scoop ¼ cup into a separate bowl and set aside. Spoon the remaining frosting into a zip-top plastic bag and cut ⅛ inch off the tip.

Following the triangle edges, pipe a darker blue line to start forming the collar, stopping at the tip of the triangle. Repeat the same line on the left side but extend it by ¾ inch where the collar overlaps. Pipe lines all around the collar, as shown, including over the scored lines made earlier. Fill in the collar with thin lines, and lightly smooth the frosting. Cut another ⅛ inch off the tip of the bag and pipe over the same collar outline to define the edges.

Using a skewer, score two lines down the cake to make the button panel. Pipe a dark blue line over the right scored line. Pipe an outline around the top edge of the cake, including the sleeve seams, and then pipe around the gray shirt openings. Set the cake aside.

5 make the flowers

Holding 1 marshmallow vertically, cut it in half diagonally. On each half, make 3 evenly spaced diagonal cuts to form different sized petals; set aside the corner pieces. Group the petal sizes without letting the pieces touch. Repeat with 4 more marshmallows. (Dust your fingers with cornstarch if the marshmallows get too sticky.) You should have 10 petal slices in each of the 3 groups and a collection of corner pieces.

Starting with the largest petals, arrange two 5-petal flowers on your work surface without the petals touching, and decide which ends will face inside the flower. To alter the petal shape, pinch one side. Repeat for the medium and small petals until you have 2 flowers of each size.

In a bowl, tint 2 tablespoons vanilla frosting yellow. Using a #4 round paintbrush, brush the frosting on the bottom third of each petal. Arrange the flowers on the shirt, one petal at a time, with the petals slightly overlapping. Arrange the petals and flowers in a pattern you find appealing, using the photo as a guide. Brush yellow frosting on the bottom third of 3 of the nicest corner pieces and place those as well.

Slice the remaining 2 marshmallows as before, separating them into groups, and frosting the bottom third of the petals yellow. Use these petals to create partial flowers on the sides of the shirt, including the outer sleeves and torso.

6 add the leaves and stems

Using scissors, cut the length of the sticks of Wrigley's Spearmint gum in half and cut them into wide leaves with pointy ends. Arrange the leaves on the flowers as shown, including the side flowers. Take the reserved ¼ cup blue frosting, add ¼ cup vanilla frosting, and add enough yellow food coloring to create a green shade. Spoon the green frosting into a zip-top plastic bag and make a pinhole-size cut at the tip. Use this to pipe the squiggly stems on all the flowers.

Cut ⅛ inch more off the tip of the frosting bag, and outline all the leaves; then pipe a center line half the length of each leaf.

7 make the buttons

In a small bowl, stir 2 tablespoons vanilla frosting until smooth. Spoon this into a zip-top plastic bag and cut ¼ inch off the tip. Starting at the top of the shirt, pipe 6 large dots, evenly spaced, down the front. Pipe 6 smaller gray dots on the white dots to finish the buttons.

8 add the sand

In a bowl, combine the vanilla wafers and sugar. Sprinkle the mixture all around the cake, using your hands to smooth out the sand.

caterpillar

We are crazy about this adorable caterpillar with its infectious smile. The pretty pastel colors make it a perfect cake for any springtime event, when new pale green shoots are coming up out of the ground and flowers are bursting into life at every turn.

caterpillar

SERVES 50
LEVEL OF DIFFICULTY: 2

special tools

- 1 (13 × 19-inch) cake board
- Small offset spatula
- 1-inch flat-head paintbrush
- 2 (10-inch) wooden skewers
- Wire cutters
- 1 (18-gauge) cloth- or paper-covered wire, 18 inches long

ingredients

- 5 pink Hostess Sno Balls
- 1 (12 × 16-inch) sheet cake (½ sheet) with vanilla frosting
- Betty Crocker Writing Icing: blue, pink, and yellow
- 2 flower-shaped thin ginger cookies (we use Anna's Ginger Thins)
- 4½ cups vanilla frosting (3 16-ounce cans)
- Liquid food coloring: green, yellow, pink, and blue
- 1¼ cups shredded sweetened coconut
- ½ (20-ounce) carton machine gumball refills in assorted colors (about 100 gumballs)
- 1 (2-ounce) package Sour Punch Straws, Green Apple flavor
- 1 marshmallow
- 2 purple Chewy Spree candies or regular Sprees
- 1 Haribo Wheel, black licorice flavor
- 2 red jujubes
- 1 candy necklace
- 8 Tootsie Pop Drops, orange flavor (from 2 to 3 2.5-ounce packages)
- 11 sticks Wrigley's Spearmint gum
- 1 tablespoon decorating confetti sprinkles, rainbow color

1 prepare the cake

Before starting, put the Sno Balls in the refrigerator to firm up.

Remove the frosting decorations from the sheet cake and trim the cake board (see pages 14 and 15). Put the cake, on its trimmed board, on a 13 × 19-inch cake board and attach with glue. Refrigerate the cake.

2 make the cookie flowers

Using the blue and pink writing icing, pipe a blue circle on 1 ginger cookie in the area just below the petals, and pipe a pink circle on a second cookie. Outline each petal on the blue cookie with the yellow icing; outline each petal on the pink cookie with the blue icing. Gently set the cookies aside.

3 frost the cake

In a bowl, tint 3¼ cups plus 2 tablespoons vanilla frosting light green using a 2-to-1 ratio of green and yellow food coloring. Using an offset spatula, frost the cake green. Dip the spatula in hot water, shake off the excess, and carefully smooth the frosting. Clean up the board and refrigerate the cake.

4 make the caterpillar body

Put ½ cup of the shredded coconut in a bowl, and put ¼ cup in each of 3 other bowls. Using liquid food coloring, tint the ½ cup of coconut pink, tossing the coconut

vigorously with your hands until it is well coated. Of the remaining 3 bowls of coconut, tint one blue, one yellow, and one purple (use equal amounts blue and pink liquid food coloring). Holding one of the chilled Sno Balls, frost it with vanilla frosting. Sprinkle and press the pink coconut on top, covering the dome completely, and put it on a large plate. Repeat with the remaining Sno Balls so that you have 2 pink, 1 blue, 1 yellow, and 1 purple. Refrigerate.

5 finish the cookie flowers

Use the writing icings to fill in the blue and pink flower centers. On the blue flower, fill in the yellow petal outlines with pink icing, and on the pink flower, fill in the blue petal outlines with yellow icing. Set aside.

6 start the grass

In a bowl, tint the remaining light green frosting a darker shade with more green food coloring. Using a 1-inch paintbrush, brush the darker green frosting on all sides of the cake with random horizontal strokes. Be careful not to cover too much of the lighter green. Dip an offset spatula in hot water, shake off the excess, and carefully glide it over the frosting to create depth and shading in the grass.

7 make a border around the cake

Make a gumball border around the bottom of the cake using assorted colors. Make a border on the top of the cake by lining up green Sour Punch Straws, cutting to fit.

8 make the caterpillar

Put the purple Sno Ball 3½ inches from the bottom edge and ½ inch from the right edge of the cake. Referring to the photo, stagger the other Sno Balls as shown. For the caterpillar head, put the second pink Sno Ball on its side, flat side forward, staggered ½ inch below the blue segment. To secure the head, push a skewer straight through the top to the bottom of the cake; cut it flush with wire cutters, and sprinkle some pink coconut to hide the hole.

In a bowl, tint 2 tablespoons vanilla frosting pink. Using an offset spatula, frost the caterpillar's face. Cut two ¼-inch-thick circles from the ends of a marshmallow and put them on the face as eyes. For the eyeballs, attach 2 purple Chewy Sprees with a little frosting, holding the back of the head while you press them into the marshmallows. Unravel a 2½-inch-long piece of black licorice wheel for the mouth. Add 2 red jujubes as dimples.

Cut the wire into two 7-inch-long pieces. Push the wire pieces into the head in a "V," leaving 3 inches exposed. Thread pieces of the candy necklace onto each antenna, leaving ¼ inch of wire exposed. Pierce 2 dark purple gumballs with a skewer, pushing it about ¼ inch deep, and put the gumballs on top of the antennae.

Below each body segment, center 2 orange Tootsie Pop Drops about ¼ inch apart as feet.

9 place the cookie flowers

Put each flower on the cake as shown, or in a spot you find appealing. Prop up each flower with a green gumball for support.

10 finish the grass details

Cut ¾ inch off each of the Wrigley's Spearmint gum sticks and discard the trimmings. Cut each stick into a leaf shape with scissors, saving the trimmings. Holding the gum vertically, lightly pinch the bottom third, folding the two sides together. Curve the sides in toward each other so the gum resembles a shovel. Push the blades into the grass in a random pattern. Push the saved trimmings into the cake as well, and sprinkle the confetti over the grass.

lawn mower

Impress all the neighbors with your brand-new lawn mower. Bigger is better when it comes to machinery, and yours has some of the best parts around. A solid body of pound cake, monster-size Peppermint Pattie wheels, and a Ding Dong on top will make you the king of your hill!

SERVES 25

LEVEL OF DIFFICULTY: 2.5

special tools

- 1 (9 × 13-inch) cake board
  Small offset spatula
- 4 (6-inch) cardboard cake circles
  #4 round artist's paintbrush
  Wire cutters
- 1 (18- to 22-gauge) cloth- or
  paper-covered wire, 18 inches long

ingredients

- 1 (8 × 12-inch) sheet cake (¼ sheet)
  with vanilla frosting
- 3¾ cups vanilla frosting
  (2½ 16-ounce cans)
- Paste or gel paste food coloring:
  green, yellow, red, and black
  (SEE SOURCES, PAGE 201)
- 1 tablespoon chocolate frosting (from
  1 16-ounce can)
- ¼ cup chocolate melting wafers (SEE
  SOURCES, PAGE 201)
- 4 (1.4-ounce) York Peppermint Patties
- 4 purple Giant Chewy SweeTarts
  (from 4 1.5-ounce packages)
- 1 (10.75-ounce) frozen pound cake
  (we use Sara Lee), thawed
- 8 wafer cookies (each 2½ inches
  long)
- 1 Ding Dong
- 1 Oreo Cakester
- 2 purple Spree candies
- 2 purple jujubes
- 1 large black or purple gumdrop
- 1 Haribo Wheel, black licorice flavor
- 2 ropes Twizzlers Pull 'n' Peel, cherry
  flavor
- 3 black licorice Twizzlers
- 2 (2-ounce) packages Sour Punch
  Straws, Green Apple flavor
- 7 sticks Wrigley's Spearmint gum

1 prepare the cake

Remove the frosting decorations from the sheet cake and trim the cake board (see pages 14 and 15). Put the cake, on its trimmed board, on a 9 × 13-inch cake board and attach with glue.

In a bowl, tint 1½ cups vanilla frosting green using a 1-to-1 ratio of green to yellow food coloring, and then mix in the chocolate frosting. Using an offset spatula, frost the cake. Dip the spatula in hot water, shake off the excess, and carefully smooth the frosting. Clean up the board and refrigerate the cake until the frosting is firm, about 30 minutes.

2 make the lawn mower

In a microwave-safe bowl, melt the chocolate wafers at 10-second intervals, stirring until smooth. Spoon the chocolate into a zip-top plastic bag and cut ⅛ inch off the tip. To make the wheels, pipe a pea-size amount of chocolate on the back center of each of 4 Peppermint Patties, and put 1 purple Giant SweeTart on top of the chocolate. Slice ¼ inch off one side of each Peppermint Pattie to flatten it, and set the wheels aside.

To make the lawn mower body, lightly trim the top of the pound cake to make it flat, and remove the side crusts. Trim equal amounts off each end to make a 5-inch-long cake. In a bowl, tint ½ cup vanilla frosting red. Scoop 2 tablespoons of the frosting into a separate bowl for crumb-coating. Put the pound cake onto a 6-inch cardboard cake circle. Using an offset spatula, crumb-coat the cake with a thin layer of red frosting. Clean up the cake circle and refrigerate the cake.

In a bowl, tint ½ cup vanilla frosting gray using black food coloring. Scoop 2 tablespoons of the frosting into a separate bowl for crumb-coating. Attach 4 wafer cookies side by side with a thin layer of frosting in between. Attach the block of wafer cookies to a 6-inch cardboard cake circle with frosting. Make another block of 4 wafers and attach it on top of the first one. Cut the cardboard around the perimeter of the wafers with scissors, and then put it onto another 6-inch cake circle. Crumb-coat the wafers. Clean up the cake circle and refrigerate.

Slice ¼ inch off 2 sides of a Ding Dong. Cut an Oreo Cakester in half through the filling, and put one of the halves, filling side down, on top of the Ding Dong; discard the other half. Put it onto a 6-inch cake circle and crumb-coat it with gray frosting. Clean up the cake circle and refrigerate.

Take the lawn mower body and frost it red. Smooth the frosting, clean up the cake circle, and refrigerate.

Take the wafer piece and frost it gray. Smooth the frosting, clean up the cake circle, and refrigerate. Repeat the process with the Ding Dong piece, frosting it gray, and refrigerate.

3 start the grass

Take the remaining green frosting and tint it a darker shade using more green food coloring. On the sheet cake, lightly spread the dark green frosting in random strokes over the lighter green frosting, leaving areas exposed underneath. Refrigerate for 15 minutes.

4 assemble the lawn mower

Using your hand and an offset spatula, put the lawn mower body on the sheet cake, centering it lengthwise 2 inches from the left. Center the gray wafer piece, with its trimmed cardboard attached, lengthwise on top of the lawn mower base. Put the Ding Dong piece on top of the gray wafer section with the flat sides on the same sides as the wheels.

Tint the remaining gray frosting black using black food coloring. Using a #4 paintbrush, brush black frosting over the chocolate-covered areas of the Peppermint Pattie wheels, and set them aside on a sheet of wax paper.

Spoon the remaining black frosting into a zip-top plastic bag and cut ⅛ inch off the tip. Pipe a bottom and top border around the wafer section, and a top border around the Ding Dong. Put a purple Spree on the front left and right sides of the wafer section, and 2 jujubes on the two back corners. Pipe a border around each Spree, 3 diagonal lines on both sides, and 3 dots on each side.

On the top of the Ding Dong piece, pipe a semicircle and a large dot. Cut the thickness of 1 large black or purple gumdrop in half and center the flat half against the back of the wafer section. Pipe 1 dot on each side of the gumdrop. Cut a black licorice wheel in half and put one half on each flat side of the Ding Dong piece, cut side down. Pipe 3 horizontal lines to the sides of the licorice wheels.

5 attach the wheels

Position the wheels, flat edge down, on the body of the lawn mower as shown. Using black frosting, pipe 1 dot in the center of the purple SweeTart on each wheel and 5 dots around it. At the base of all sides of the lawn mower, put a piece of the Twizzlers Pull 'n' Peel rope between the wheels, cutting to fit. Loop two 3-inch-long strands of the Pull 'n' Peel in an upside-down "U," and put them on the sides between the wheels. Cut to fit.

6 make the handle

Cut ¼ inch off each end of 3 black Twizzlers to expose the holes. Set 1 Twizzler aside. Using wire cutters, cut the wire in half and lightly wet it. Thread the wire through one of the Twizzlers until one end of the Twizzler is flush with one end of the wire. Repeat for the second Twizzler. Push the exposed wire ends into the lawn mower body at a 45-degree angle up to but not through the bottom of the wafer section.

For the top of the handle, cut the remaining black Twizzler to the distance between the wired Twizzlers. Re-melt the chocolate for 10 seconds or until smooth. Connect the long arms of the handle to the shorter piece with a dot of chocolate on each end. Pipe a black dot on both ends of the small Twizzler piece.

7 finish the grass

In a bowl, tint ½ cup vanilla frosting light green using equal amounts green and yellow food coloring. Spoon the frosting into a zip-top plastic bag and cut ¹⁄₁₆ inch off the tip. Pipe squiggly lines over the cake, except in the rear path of the lawn mower, keeping in mind that you want to see some of the grass layer below.

8 finish the cake

Line the bottom edges of the cake with the green Sour Punch Straws, cutting to fit. Cut the sticks of gum in half and cut the halves into leaf shapes, saving the trimmings. Cut the leaves in half lengthwise to make blades of grass, and put these and the trimmings around all sides of the cake.

aquarium

"Under the sea" themed cakes are perennial favorites, and our version is a real showstopper. We decided to give the aquarium extra height by stacking the sheet cake: you cut in half to form two cakes, then stack one on top of the other. We filled our aquarium with the marine life we love, but you can put any kinds of creatures you like in yours.

SERVES 50
LEVEL OF DIFFICULTY: 1.5

special tools

- 1 (13 × 19-inch) cake board
- 4 drinking straws
- Large offset spatula
- Small offset spatula
- Small rolling pin
- Small pizza cutter
- ½-inch flat-head paintbrush

ingredients

- 1 (12 × 16-inch) sheet cake (½ sheet) with vanilla frosting
- 4¾ cups plus 2 tablespoons vanilla frosting (3¼ 16-ounce cans)
- Paste or gel paste food coloring: blue and black (SEE SOURCES, PAGE 201)
- 1½ cups Fruity Pebbles cereal
- 1 (2-ounce) bag Gold Mine Nugget Bubble Gum
- Cornstarch, for dusting
- 5 Spearmint Leaves candy
- 8 Jolly Rancher Fruit Chews: 4 green apple flavor and 4 cherry flavor
- 4 tropical fish gummi candies
- 10 Haribo Clown Fish gummi candies
- ½ cup ground vanilla wafers
- ¼ cup granulated sugar

① prepare the cake

Remove the frosting decorations from the sheet cake and trim the cake board (see pages 14 and 15).

Put the cake in front of you horizontally. Measure its length with a ruler, and then cut its width in half. You need to cut through the cake board as well, by pulling the cake and board over the edge of the counter to the line where the cake is divided. Holding the extended half of the cake underneath for support, cut through the board with the other hand, using a serrated knife with a sawing motion.

Put one of the cakes, on its trimmed board, in the center of a 13 × 19-inch cake board and attach it with glue. Push 4 drinking straws evenly spaced into the cake and cut them just below the frosting. Create a grid pattern with the straws: 4 across and 3 down, for a total of 12, within ¾ inch of any edge. Put the second cake, on its trimmed board, on top of the first. Be sure to look for any unevenness and position the cakes so that the top is level.

② frost the cake

In a bowl, tint 3 cups vanilla frosting light blue. Scoop ½ cup of the frosting into a separate bowl for crumb-coating. Crumb-coat any unfrosted sides of the cake with a thin layer of frosting. Refrigerate until the frosting is firm, about 20 minutes.

Using a large offset spatula, frost the cake light blue. Dip the spatula in hot water, shake off the excess, and carefully smooth the frosting. Refrigerate until firm, about 30 minutes.

Tint the remaining blue frosting (adding more if necessary to make 1 cup) a darker shade by adding more blue food coloring. Using a small offset spatula, apply some of the darker blue frosting on all sides and the top of the cake, lightly smearing it and leaving some lighter blue areas exposed. Smooth the frosting.

③ add the rocks and gravel

Sprinkle Fruity Pebbles cereal on the lower part of the top surface of the cake, creating an uneven terrain with dips and peaks. Sprinkle the Gold Nugget gum over the cereal for more texture.

With your hands, lightly press Fruity Pebbles cereal onto the bottom third of all sides of the cake, no higher than 1½ inches. Use the back side of the small spatula to lightly press the cereal into the cake. Randomly arrange the Gold Nugget pieces in the cereal.

④ make the seaweed

Make the spearmint-colored seaweed pieces first: Dust a work surface with cornstarch and roll out 5 Spearmint Leaves until they are 5 inches long. Using a pizza cutter, cut them into long leaf shapes, tapered on both sides. Using scissors, cut two-thirds of the way down the middle of the leaves. Plant 1 seaweed into the cereal mixture on the top right side, and plant the other 4 seaweeds vertically on the corners of the cake, lightly twisting the leaves.

To make the 4 lime-green seaweeds, mash each green apple Jolly Rancher Fruit Chew into a cylinder. Add more cornstarch to your work surface and roll out the fruit chews into thin strips. Cut them into long leaf shapes similar to the other seaweed. Cut a sliver down 3 of the seaweed pieces to about 1 inch from the bottom, and lightly twist the pieces. For the seaweed that will go on the top center, cut the piece on both sides and lightly twist it.

Plant each piece of seaweed into the cereal mixture as before. Use the photo as a guide for arranging the seaweed.

5 make the red coral

Cut each of the cherry Jolly Rancher Fruit Chews in half and lightly form them into cylinders. Then push the end of the paintbrush handle into each cylinder to make a hole. Put the coral, holes facing upward, on the top of the cake tucked next to some seaweed. Vary the height of the coral pieces for a more realistic scene.

6 make a border around the cake

Fill a zip-top plastic bag with the darker blue frosting and cut ¼ inch off the tip. Use the back of an offset spatula to gently push some of the cereal away from the top edge, and pipe a border around the cake.

CONTINUES ➡

7 add the fish

Arrange all the tropical gummi fish and gummi clown fish on the surface of the cake using the photo as a guide, or as desired. Spoon ¼ cup vanilla frosting into a zip-top plastic bag and cut ⅛ inch off the tip. Squeeze a small eyeball onto each of the clown fish. If your tropical gummi fish do not already have eyes, add them as well.

Tint ⅓ cup vanilla frosting black. Spoon the frosting into a plastic bag and cut ⅛ inch off the tip. Pipe a small black pupil over the white eyeball on each fish. On each clown fish, pipe a black line between the white and colored sections. Cut another ⅛ inch off the tip of the bag, and pipe a black border over the dark blue border around the cake.

8 make the bubbles

Using the bag of vanilla frosting, pipe varying-sized bubbles above each fish on the cake. Balance the scene on the surface with a few extra piped bubbles where needed. Squeeze the remaining darker blue frosting into another plastic bag and cut ⅛ inch off the tip. Pipe a small blue dot on each of the bubbles.

9 add the sand

In a bowl, combine the vanilla wafers and sugar. Spoon the sand mixture around the cake as evenly as possible.

watering can

The next time you want to send flowers, consider giving a gift of a lovely watering can cake bursting with colorful blooms instead. This cake was inspired by those vintage metal watering cans that have elegant long spouts. When you're forming the flowers, it is best to keep the Fruit Roll-ups cold and work with them one at a time from the refrigerator. The pieces become more challenging as they get warm.

SERVES 15

LEVEL OF DIFFICULTY: 3

special tools

- **Small offset spatula**
- **1 (14 × 16-inch) cake board**
- **½-inch flat-head paintbrush**

ingredients

- **5 Sunkist Fruit Gems: 3 yellow and 2 red**
- **2 flower-shaped thin ginger cookies (we use Anna's Ginger Thins)**
- **Betty Crocker Writing Icing: yellow and purple**
- **2 (16-ounce) frozen pound cakes (we use Sara Lee family-size), thawed**
- **2 large (2.25-ounce) Tootsie Rolls (6 inches long each)**
- **3 cups vanilla frosting (2 16-ounce cans)**
- **Paste or gel paste food coloring: pink and green** (SEE SOURCES, PAGE 201)
- **2 green Twizzlers Rainbow Twists**
- **2 Twinkies**
- **6 Betty Crocker Blastin' Berry Hot Colors Fruit Roll-ups, Sizzling Red/Yellow flavor**
- **6 Betty Crocker Blastin' Berrry Hot Colors Fruit Roll-ups, Blazin' Blue/Green flavor**
- **6 sticks Wrigley's Spearmint gum**
- **1 Nutter Butter cookie**
- **1 red Dot**
- **1 Sour Punch Straw, strawberry flavor**
- **1 strip Necco Candy Buttons**

1 decorate the cookies

Attach a yellow Sunkist Fruit Gem to the center of each ginger cookie, using the yellow writing icing. Outline the petals on both flowers with the yellow icing. Carefully set the cookies aside.

2 shape the watering can

Lightly trim the tops of the pound cakes to make them flat, and remove the side crusts. Put the cakes together vertically, side by side, on a work surface. Cut equal amounts off both the top and bottom to make the cakes 8 inches long; reserve the trimmings.

3 make the spout

Cut a 1½-inch-wide strip off the entire right side of the cake. Trim the cut-off strip to 1 inch wide, discarding the trimmings. Put it horizontally on the work surface. Make a mark on the top edge of the strip 1½ inches from the left end. Line up the knife at an angle between the mark and the bottom left corner, and cut through, discarding the trimming. Make a mark on the bottom edge 1½ inches from the right end. Line up the knife at an angle between the mark and the top right corner, and cut through.

Put the body of the watering can vertically on a 14 × 16-inch cake board, placing it 1½ inches from the bottom edge and 5 inches from the right side. Put the spout against the right side of the can. Take the reserved trimmings from Step 2 and center the rounded side of one piece at the end of the spout. Put the second trimming on the top of the can, flush right, with the rounded side facing up.

4 make the handle

Stack the Tootsie Rolls on top of each other. Curve them until the ends are 5 inches apart, and put them flush against the left side of the watering can, centered. Once the watering can pieces fit well on the board, remove the handle with an offset spatula and set it aside on a piece of wax paper on a plate.

5 frost the cake

In a bowl, tint 2¼ cups vanilla frosting pink. Scoop ½ cup of the frosting into a separate bowl for crumb-coating. Using the crumb-coat frosting, attach the cake pieces to each other and to the board. Crumb-coat the cake. Refrigerate the cake until the frosting is firm, 20 to 25 minutes.

Wipe any crumbs from the Tootsie Roll handle. Use a ½-inch flat-head paintbrush to brush the handle with pink frosting, completely covering it. Refrigerate for about 15 minutes. Add a second and then a third coat of frosting, refrigerating between frostings.

Using an offset spatula, frost the cake pink. Dip the spatula in hot water, shake off the excess, and carefully smooth the frosting. Clean up the board and refrigerate until firm, about 30 minutes.

When both pieces are firm, put the handle in place on the left side of the watering can.

CONTINUES ➡

6 add the frosting details

In a bowl, tint ⅓ cup vanilla frosting a darker pink using more food coloring. Spoon it into a zip-top plastic bag and cut ¼ inch off the tip. Pipe a border around all edges of the cake, on the top and bottom, and over the seams where the pieces connect. Just below the seam connecting the curved piece at the top of the watering can, pipe 1 large dot at each corner and 7 small dots in between. On the bottom right corner, where the spout meets the can, pipe 2 large dots with 4 small dots in between. Pipe 1 large dot on each end of the handle. Refrigerate the cake.

7 make the flowers

Take the reserved flower cookies and fill in the petals with purple writing icing. Carefully set aside.

For the stems, cut 3 pieces out of 2 green Twizzlers to the following lengths: 4 inches, 3½ inches, and 3 inches. Put the 3½-inch piece on the board in the center of the can opening.

Angle the 4-inch piece to the left and the 3-inch piece to the right.

Cut the length of one of the Twinkies in half. Put both pieces, flat side down, on the board with the rounded ends meeting the middle stem and the right-hand stem. Put 1 yellow Sunkist Fruit Gem on the cream side of the left Twinkie, and 1 red Fruit Gem on the cream side of the right one.

Take one of the red/yellow Fruit Roll-ups, and use scissors or a knife to separate the two colors. To form the rose shape, wrap the yellow piece over the left-hand Twinkie while slightly wrinkling it, leaving a ¼-inch lip beyond the top. Repeat with the red piece on the other Twinkie. Separate a second red/yellow Fruit Roll-up and wrap the yellow piece in the same manner, ¼ inch below the first piece. Repeat with the second red piece on the other flower. Add a third piece of each color to the flowers, molding this last piece to the rounded Twinkie ends.

Separate 1 blue/green Fruit Roll-up, and set aside the blue piece. Cut the green piece in half diagonally to make 2 leaves. Take 1 piece and pinch the short side of the triangle together. Put the leaf against the left side of the left-hand stem, bending it to the left. Repeat for the red rose, to the right of the stem.

Cover 1 inch of the top of the left stem with 1 purple daisy cookie, attaching it with a little frosting.

Cut the remaining Twinkie in half, and discard one half. Put the Twinkie, flat side down, rounded side to the left, against the top left side of the can. Put 1 red Sunkist Fruit Gem on the cream side of the Twinkie. To make the second red rose, repeat the same procedure as

before, using 3 more red/yellow Fruit Roll-ups, reserving the yellow parts.

Cut the sticks of gum in half; then cut each piece into a wide leaf shape. Set aside 6 leaves. Evenly space 3 leaves around the base of the top red rose. Repeat with the other 3 leaves on the yellow rose.

To make 3 blue roses, take 4 of the blue/green Fruit Roll-ups and separate the blue section, discarding the green. Working with 1 piece at a time, loosely fold the piece in half lengthwise, and roll it up to form a rose shape, tighter on the bottom and more open on top. Continue to wrap the rose with a second blue piece, and then pinch the bottom of the roll-up. Put the blue rose in the corner of the

can above the handle. Repeat the process to make a second blue rose to put between the red roses. For the third blue rose, use the last blue Roll-up, putting it below the other blue rose.

Take the 3 reserved yellow Fruit Roll-up pieces, and repeat the above procedure, making one yellow rose with 2 pieces and the second with 1 piece. Put the larger rose below the 2 blue roses, face up. The second yellow rose sits below the right red rose. Center the second daisy cookie over the left corner of the can.

Use the photo as a guide to place the 6 remaining gum leaves. In a bowl, tint ¼ cup vanilla frosting dark green, and spoon it into a zip-top plastic bag. Cut ¹⁄₁₆ inch off the tip. Pipe vines

around the flowers, as shown. Cut another ¹⁄₁₆ inch off the tip and pipe a line halfway down the center of each gum leaf.

⑧ make the butterfly

Open the Nutter Butter cookie and scrape off the filling. Put the 2 halves, smooth side out, on the cake on the lower left side and slightly angled together. Using the dark pink frosting, pipe an outline on the wings and a line down the center. Put 1 red Dot as the head and cut 1 red Sour Punch Straw to fit the middle of the body. Attach the yellow and pink Necco candy buttons to the cookie with frosting. To finish, pipe the pink antennae.

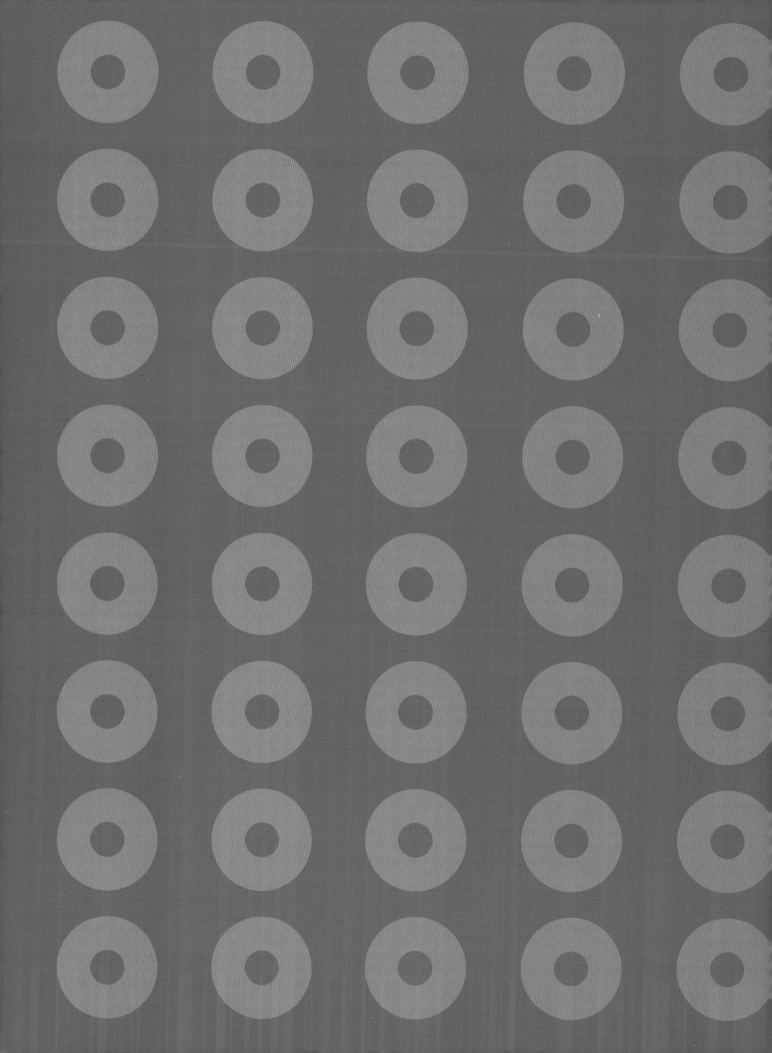

holiday FUN

snowman

Our favorite classic Christmas television special when we were growing up was *Frosty the Snowman*. It's clear that the lovable snowman inspired this cute and festive cake that kids of all ages will fall for. If you are working in a cold climate, you may want to warm up the Tootsie Rolls in the microwave for a few seconds before forming the snowman's arms.

snowman

SERVES 60
LEVEL OF DIFFICULTY: 2.5

special tools

- 1 (13 × 19-inch) cake board
  Small offset spatula
- 4 (6-inch) cardboard cake circles
- 1 (8-inch) cardboard cake circle
- ½-inch flat-head paintbrush
- #4 round artist's paintbrush
- 6 round toothpicks
- 3 (10-inch) wooden skewers
  Wire cutters

ingredients

- 1 (12 × 16-inch) sheet cake (½ sheet) with vanilla frosting
- 5¼ cups vanilla frosting (3½ 16-ounce cans)
- 3 (16-ounce) frozen pound cakes (we use Sara Lee family-size), thawed
- 1⅓ cups shredded sweetened coconut, chopped
- Paste or gel paste food coloring: black and blue (SEE SOURCES, PAGE 201)
- 1 (1.4-ounce) York Peppermint Pattie
- 1 Hostess CupCake, any flavor
- 1 (16-ounce) package Twizzlers, strawberry flavor
- 3 peppermint Life Savers
- 1 candy necklace
- 11 marshmallows
- 1 Sour Punch Straw, strawberry flavor
- 1 large orange gumdrop
- 2 black round Jujyfruits
- 1 Haribo Wheel, black licorice flavor
- 1 Fruit by the Foot, strawberry flavor
- Liquid food coloring: black
- Pure lemon extract
- 3 Necco Wafers
- 1 large (2.25-ounce) Tootsie Roll (6 inches long)

① prepare the cake

Remove the frosting decorations from the sheet cake and trim the cake board (see pages 14 and 15). Put the cake, on its trimmed board, on a 13 × 19-inch cake board and attach with glue.

In a medium bowl, stir 3 cups of vanilla frosting until smooth; then frost the cake with an offset spatula. Dip the spatula in hot water, shake off the excess, and carefully smooth the frosting. Clean up the board and refrigerate the cake.

② shape and frost the snowman

Lightly trim the tops of the pound cakes to make them flat, and remove the side crusts. Put 2 cakes side by side horizontally on a work surface; set the third cake aside. Center a 6-inch cardboard cake circle on top of the cakes, and using it as a stencil, cut out a circle; discard the trimmings. This will be the body piece. Take the reserved pound cake and cut it in half widthwise. Put the pieces side by side horizontally on a work surface. Using a lid from a frosting can as a stencil, cut out a circle; discard the trimmings. This will be the head.

Put 1 cup vanilla frosting in a bowl to frost the snowman, and separate ¼ cup into another bowl to be used for snow. Using the frosting, attach the pieces of the 6-inch round cake to each other and to a 6-inch cardboard circle. Repeat with the pieces of the 3-inch cake. Using scissors, cut off the excess cardboard around the 2 cake circles. Keeping the trimmed cardboard pieces attached, put the 6-inch

cake on an 8-inch cake circle and the 3-inch cake on a 6-inch cake circle. Using a knife, round off the top edges of both cakes by trimming ¼ inch all the way around.

Using an offset spatula, lightly frost both of the cakes with vanilla frosting. Cover the cakes with the coconut. Set aside.

③ start making the hat

In a bowl, tint ¼ cup vanilla frosting black using black paste food coloring. Cut ½ inch off one side of a Peppermint Pattie. Using a ½-inch flat-head paintbrush, brush the entire surface, except the cut edge, with black frosting. Put it on a piece of wax paper and refrigerate.

Put a Hostess CupCake, frosting side up, on a work surface and cut ¼ inch off one side. Put it, cut side down, on a 6-inch cardboard cake circle and frost it black with the offset spatula. Carefully smooth the frosting. Clean up the cardboard and refrigerate.

④ make the sky

In a bowl, tint ½ cup vanilla frosting sky blue. Position the sheet cake vertically, and use a skewer to score a slightly arced horizon line 7 inches from the bottom on both sides. Lightly frost the portion above the horizon line sky blue.

Spoon the reserved ¼ cup vanilla frosting into a zip-top plastic bag. Cut ¼ inch off the tip, and pipe a white line along the scored horizon line. Around the top and bottom edges of the cake, make a border of Strawberry Twizzlers, and cut to fit.

5 assemble the snowman

Take the 6-inch round cake, with the cardboard base attached, and place the body of the snowman on the sheet cake, centered and 2½ inches from the bottom so that the snowman's head will lie above the horizon line. Center the head, with its cut cardboard base, above the body.

6 assemble the hat

To make the hat brim, take the frosted Peppermint Pattie and insert 2 toothpicks one third of the way into the cut side. Put the Pattie flush against the head of the snowman and push it down, inserting the toothpicks into the sheet cake. Put the frosted cupcake, cut side down, on the Pattie with the narrow side against the hat brim.

7 decorate the sheet cake

Put 3 Life Savers and 5 of the white candy necklace pieces on the sky as shown in the photo. Squeeze the vanilla frosting into another plastic bag and cut ⅛ inch off the tip. Pipe the snowflake lines around each of the candy pieces, 4 long and 4 short. Pipe a dot at the end of each line.

Cut 5 of the marshmallows in half and scatter them, along with the remaining marshmallows, evenly over the snow area.

8 decorate the snowman

Make a ribbon on the hat by running 1 red Sour Punch Straw around the top of the brim, and cut to fit. Add the nose by inserting a toothpick into the bottom of a large orange gumdrop and inserting it, centered, 1½ inches from the bottom of the face. Make the eyes by inserting toothpicks into 2 round black Jujyfruits and adding them above the nose, ½ inch apart. Cut a 3½-inch piece off the black licorice wheel to make the mouth.

To make the scarf, cut a 16-inch-long piece of the Fruit by the Foot. Cut it in half to make two 8-inch pieces. On one end of each 8-inch piece, make small cuts to create fringe. Starting at the back of the neck on the left side, drape one piece of the scarf down over the body. Fold the scarf, if needed, to help it fit snug to the neck. Drape the second piece around the other side of the neck. At the point where the pieces cross, use a #4 paintbrush to brush water between them to help them stick. Cut off the remaining piece. Reposition the cut piece so that it points to the right and attach it with water. To make it look like the scarf is floating, insert a toothpick at an angle under the fringe end of the relocated piece.

To form the knot, cut a 1¾-inch-long piece of Fruit by the Foot and fold each end under by ¼ inch. Wet the 2 folded sides and attach the knot vertically where the cut pieces meet on the scarf.

Lay down a piece of wax paper. In a small bowl, mix ¼ teaspoon each of liquid black food coloring and lemon extract. Using a #4 paintbrush, brush the black coloring on the unprinted sides and edges of the 3 Necco Wafers. Let dry for a few minutes. Put the Neccos in a vertical line below the scarf as buttons. Using white frosting, pipe a dot in the corner of the snowman's eyes, and pipe a curved line on each of the black buttons for accents.

9 make the arms

Cut the Tootsie Roll in half. Cut off 3 inches from the flat ends of 2 skewers. Insert the pointed end of a skewer through the length of one Tootsie Roll. Repeat with the second skewer and Tootsie Roll. Form each arm so it is slightly tapered on the end where the skewer sticks out. Make 2 cuts with scissors, no longer than ¾ inch, at the other end to make 3 evenly sized fingers. Just before serving the cake, insert the arms into the body.

valentine's roses

The timeless beauty of a dozen red roses symbolizes love and appreciation. If you can't decide whether to give roses or sweets, why not give both! Every piece on the cake is edible, including the ribbon. She can have her flowers, cake, and candy—and eat all of it, too.

valentine's roses

SERVES 20 TO 25

LEVEL OF DIFFICULTY: 2.5

special tools

- 1 (9 × 13-inch) cake board
- Small offset spatula
- 1 (8-inch) cardboard cake circle
- #4 round artist's paintbrush
- 5 round toothpicks

ingredients

- 1 (8 × 12-inch) sheet cake (¼ sheet) with vanilla frosting
- 3 cups vanilla frosting (2 16-ounce cans)
- 1 (10.75-ounce) frozen pound cake (we use Sara Lee), thawed
- Paste or gel paste food coloring: green and red (SEE SOURCES, PAGE 201)
- 1 (2-ounce) package Sour Punch Straws, green apple flavor
- 20 Betty Crocker Fruit Roll-ups, strawberry flavor
- 8 sticks Wrigley's Spearmint gum
- Pure lemon extract
- Liquid food coloring: green
- 2 rolls Betty Crocker Fruit by the Foot, strawberry flavor
- 1 (2-ounce) package Sour Punch Straws, strawberry flavor
- 2 (5-ounce) packages Haribo Wheels, strawberry flavor

① prepare the cake

Remove the frosting decorations from the sheet cake and trim the cake board (see pages 14 and 15). Put the cake, on its trimmed board, on a 9 × 13-inch cake board and attach with glue.

In a medium bowl, stir 1½ cups vanilla frosting until smooth. Using an offset spatula, frost the cake. Dip the spatula in hot water, shake off the excess, and carefully smooth the frosting. Clean up the board and refrigerate the cake.

② make the cone for the stems

Put the pound cake horizontally on a work surface. Measure 1 inch from the right and use a knife to score a line vertically across the width of the cake. Flip the cake on its side with the scored line facing you. Line up the knife on the top surface between the beginning of the scored line and the top right corner on the same surface. Cut down following the scored line, creating a wedge shape, and discard the corner.

Flip the cake back to its original position and reorient it vertically, with the wedge cut facing away from you. Find the center point of the bottom edge of the cake and make a mark. Line up the knife between the mark and the left edge of the scored line, and cut through. From the same center mark, line up the knife between the mark and the right edge of the scored line, and cut through; discard the trimmings. You should now have a triangle with the cake's top crust still intact. To round off the edges of the cuts

you just made, trim ¼ inch off the edge down the length of both sides.

Put the cake on an 8-inch cake circle. In a bowl, tint ⅓ cup vanilla frosting green using green paste food coloring. Frost the cake and smooth the frosting. Clean up the board and refrigerate until firm, about 20 minutes.

Take the cone cake and the sheet cake out of the refrigerator. Center the cone on the sheet cake, 1 inch from the bottom.

③ make the stems

Arrange 10 green Sour Punch Straws, evenly spaced, along the length of the cone and cut to fit. Fill a zip-top plastic bag with ⅓ cup of the green frosting (make more if necessary), and cut ⅛ inch off the tip. Pipe green lines between the green straws. Refrigerate the cake for 10 minutes. At the same time, refrigerate the strawberry Fruit Roll-ups.

④ make the roses

Work with 1 or 2 Fruit Roll-ups at a time, keeping the rest chilled. Of the dozen roses, 8 use 2 Roll-ups each and 4 use 1 Roll-up each. Loosely fold 1 Roll-up in half, and then roll it to form a rose shape, making it tighter on the bottom and more open on top. Repeat the process to wrap the rose with a second Roll-up. Pinch the bottom of the rose together. Put the rose, slanted to the left, on the top left of the cone. Repeat the process to make 7 more large roses, putting 3 more on the first row and 4 on the second row. For the roses in the second row, cut a small amount from the bottom to shorten them, and position them with the heads slightly forward.

For the third row, make 4 smaller roses using 1 fruit Roll-up each, and trim the length as before. Put 1 rose to the right of the second row. Put the remaining roses toward the front of the bouquet to fill in the gaps.

5 make the leaves

Cut the length of all the sticks of spearmint gum in half, and cut the halves into wide leaf shapes. Put a piece of wax paper on a work surface. In a small bowl, mix 1 teaspoon lemon extract with ½ teaspoon liquid green food coloring. Using a #4 round paintbrush, brush both sides of the leaves green. Set them on the wax paper to dry.

When dry, pinch and curve the leaves at the bottom. Nestle the leaves in between the roses.

6 make the ribbon and bow

Cut a 6½-inch piece of Fruit by the Foot and lay it across the middle of the stems. Cut it to fit, and tuck the ends under the stems. Cut 4 red Sour Punch Straws in half. Cut 3 toothpicks in half. To make the bow, bend each Sour Punch Straw to make a loop, and insert a toothpick piece halfway into each end of the loop. Insert the loop into the cake, pinching the end to prevent the toothpicks from sliding farther into the ribbon. Repeat with 5 more loops. For the last 2 pieces

of Sour Punch Straws, cut one end of each to a point, then insert 1 full toothpick halfway into the opposite end, and attach under the bow.

7 make the border

Put a line of red Sour Punch Straws around the top edge of the cake, cutting to fit. For the bottom border, unroll a Fruit by the Foot, and starting at the back of the cake, wrap it around the base, cutting to fit.

Cut the red licorice wheels in half. In a bowl, tint ⅓ cup vanilla frosting red. Spoon the frosting into a zip-top plastic bag and cut ⅛ inch off the tip. Pipe a small amount of frosting onto the back of each licorice wheel, and starting from one corner, attach the wheels, flat side down, on top of the fruit roll ribbon border. Pipe a small red dot in the hole of each wheel.

easter bunny

This cheerful cake covers all your Easter needs, from the candy to the basket, and even to the bunny! We thought hard about how to make the basket as realistic as possible and were thrilled with how great the staggered chocolate licorice twists turned out. Note that some products used in the recipe— like the pastel-colored writing icings and Easter candies—are seasonal and may be difficult to find other times of the year.

SERVES 15
LEVEL OF DIFFICULTY: 2.5

special tools

Wire cutters

2 (10-inch) wooden skewers

2 (8-inch) lollipop sticks (SEE SOURCES, PAGE 201)

1 (12 × 15-inch) cake board

Small offset spatula

½-inch flat-head paintbrush

10 to 15 round toothpicks

#4 round artist's paintbrush

ingredients

2 flower-shaped thin ginger cookies (we use Anna's Ginger Thins)

1 Nutter Butter cookie

¼ cup white chocolate melting wafers (SEE SOURCES, PAGE 201)

5 white Necco Wafers

Betty Crocker Writing Icing: pink, yellow, purple, and blue

2 (16-ounce) frozen pound cakes (we use Sara Lee family-size), thawed

1½ cups chocolate frosting (1 16-ounce can)

2 (5-ounce) packages Chocolate Twizzlers

1 Hubba Bubba Bubble Tape, Awesome Original flavor

3 large (2.25-ounce) Tootsie Rolls (each 6 inches long)

¾ cup shredded sweetened coconut

Liquid food coloring: green and yellow

1 pink Hostess Sno Ball

¾ cup vanilla frosting (½ 16-ounce can)

Paste or gel paste food coloring: pink and black (SEE SOURCES, PAGE 201)

2 Sour Punch Straws, strawberry flavor

1 red jujube

1 pink Starburst candy

3 sticks Wrigley's Doublemint gum

Pure lemon extract

13 jelly beans

5 pieces pastel candy corn

4 Whoppers Robin Eggs

① start the flowers and bunny ears

Put the flower-shaped ginger cookies, top side down, on a work surface. Split the Nutter Butter cookie in half and scrape off the filling, and put the halves on the work surface, smooth side down. Using wire cutters, cut the skewers to 6-inch lengths, preserving the pointed end.

In a microwave-safe bowl, melt the white chocolate wafers at 10-second intervals, stirring until smooth. Spoon the chocolate into a zip-top plastic bag and cut ¼ inch off the tip. Pipe a thick line of chocolate down the center of the ginger cookies, and put a lollipop stick on the chocolate, lightly pressing them together. Pipe a line of chocolate down the center of the Nutter Butter cookies, and put the skewers, pointed end down, on the chocolate, pressing them together. Set all the cookies aside until set.

Flip the flowers over and attach a white Necco Wafer to each center, using the melted chocolate as "glue." Outline the flower petals on one of the cookies with pink writing icing, and on the second cookie with yellow writing icing. Set aside to dry.

② shape the basket

Lightly trim the tops of the pound cakes to make them flat, and remove the side crusts. Cut 1 cake in half lengthwise, discarding one of the halves. Put the cake half horizontally on a work surface, cut side facing away, and put the whole pound cake in front of it. Make 2 marks on the bottom, 1 inch from the left and right corners. Line up a knife between the left mark and the top left corner and cut through. Repeat on the right side, and discard the trimmings.

In a medium bowl, stir 1 cup chocolate frosting until smooth. Using a small amount of the frosting, attach the cake pieces to each other and to a 12 × 15-inch cake board; center the cake on the board, 2 inches from the bottom. Lightly frost the cake using a small offset spatula, applying a thin layer for the body of the basket and a slightly thicker layer on the top and bottom sides.

③ decorate the basket

Line the sides of the basket with short lengths of chocolate Twizzlers, cut to fit flush with the top edge of the cake. Line the top of the basket, making sure to stagger the seams of the Twizzlers for a realistic basket-weave look. Under the basket at its base, put 1 row of Twizzlers and cut to fit.

Fill a zip-top plastic bag with 2 tablespoons chocolate frosting and cut ⅛ inch off the tip. Pipe lines over the seams of the Twizzlers on the surface and sides of the basket. Once the seams are covered, add more piped lines as needed to complete the basket weave.

Cut a 15-inch strip from the Hubba Bubba Bubble Tape. Wrap the tape around the base of the basket, ¾ inch from the bottom, and cut to fit.

4 make the handle

Working on the board, form the large Tootsie Rolls into an arc from one side of the basket top to the other.

5 make the grass

In a bowl, tint the coconut flakes green using a couple drops of liquid green food coloring, and mix thoroughly. Using an offset spatula, spread a little fresh chocolate frosting on the top of the basket to help the grass stick. Using your hands, press the coconut grass into the basket, bunching it up where the cake meets the board to give the basket a fuller appearance.

6 finish the flowers

Fill in the petals of the decorated flower cookies using the yellow and pink writing icings. Outline the Necco Wafer on the yellow flower with purple icing and then fill it in; outline the Necco Wafer on the pink flower with blue icing and fill it in. Set both flowers aside to dry.

7 make the bunny

Put the pink Sno ball ½ inch from the right side of the handle, with the flat side against the board and the bottom edge flush with the basket. In a small bowl, tint 1 tablespoon vanilla frosting pink. Using a ½-inch flat-head paintbrush, brush pink frosting on the smooth side of the Nutter Butter bunny ears, and push them into the top of the head at a slight angle, ¼ inch apart.

Fill a zip-top plastic bag with 2 tablespoons vanilla frosting and cut ⅛ inch off the tip. Pipe 2 lines side by side to outline the ears. Cut two 6-inch lengths of red Sour Punch straws and line the edges of the ears, pressing them into the vanilla frosting.

For the eyes, use a little frosting to attach 2 Necco Wafers, printed sides down, to the Sno Ball. For the nose, use half of 1 toothpick to attach a red jujube. For the mouth, cut a pink Starburst candy in half and form 2 dime-size circles. Put them side by side under the nose. For the bottom lip, take a ¾-inch piece of a red Sour Punch Straw and cut it in half lengthwise, discarding one of the halves. Curve the straw under the Starbursts, with the ends touching the Starbursts. Pipe white frosting into the mouth opening.

Tint 2 tablespoons vanilla frosting black. Spoon the frosting into a plastic bag and cut ⅛ inch off the tip. Pipe a black line inside the white line in each ear. Pipe a

½-inch circle for each pupil and fill it in. Outline the mouth from the tip of the nose halfway around each Starburst, and then outline the bottom lip. Pipe 4 black dots on each Starburst for the whiskers. Pipe 2 white curved lines on the pupils.

8 make the bow

Put the sticks of Doublemint gum on wax paper. In a bowl, mix ½ teaspoon each of lemon extract and liquid yellow food coloring. Using a #4 paintbrush, paint both sides of the gum yellow. When dry, cut the length of 1 stick in half and cut those pieces into diamond shapes. Take the 2 other sticks, make loops, and cut the ends to a point. Attach the 2 loops, pointed ends together, on the front center of the handle, using vanilla frosting as "glue." Attach the other 2 pieces in the middle of the bow, at an outward angle. Attach 1 white Necco Wafer to the bow. Using the yellow writing icing, pipe an outline around the Necco and fill it in.

9 fill the basket

Insert the 2 flowers into the left side of the basket, toward the back. Arrange the jelly beans, candy corn, and Whoppers Robin Eggs in the grass, adhering with frosting if needed. For the softer candies that aren't supported in the basket or on the board, attach them to the cake with toothpicks.

zombie

For the Halloween cake, we decided to go in a different direction from the usual pumpkins, witches, and black cats to make something that many people, including us, are fascinated with: zombies! The recipe trial stages were hilarious as Rick contemplated the best way to make an oozing brain, what to use for the zombie hair, and how to mix just the right shade of a decayed flesh tone for the face. We wanted the cake to make people laugh and slightly gross them out at the same time. Mission accomplished.

SERVES 25
LEVEL OF DIFFICULTY: 2.5

special tools

1 (13 × 19-inch) cake board

Small offset spatula

Small rolling pin

#4 round artist's paintbrush

1-inch flat-head paintbrush

½-inch flat-head paintbrush

ingredients

1 (7.25-ounce) box instant macaroni and cheese

Vegetable oil

1 (8 × 12-inch) sheet cake (¼ sheet) with chocolate frosting

1½ cups chocolate frosting (1 16-ounce can)

Cornstarch, for dusting

2 Tootsie Fruit Rolls: 1 green and 1 vanilla

8 large white gumballs

Liquid food coloring: blue, green, red, and yellow

1 (16-ounce) frozen pound cake (we use Sara Lee family-size), thawed

3 cups vanilla frosting (2 16-ounce cans)

Paste or gel paste food coloring: black (SEE SOURCES, PAGE 201)

1 individual vanilla pudding cup

5 pieces Trident White gum

2 (2.12-ounce) Big League Chew packs, Ground Ball Grape flavor

1 rope Twizzlers Pull 'n' Peel, cherry flavor

1 individual strawberry Jell-O cup

1 (5-ounce) bag gummi worms

15 to 20 whole Oreo cookies, blended in a food processor

1 prepare the macaroni

Cook the macaroni according to the package directions, discarding the cheese mixture. Strain, and toss lightly in vegetable oil. Set aside 1 cup of noodles.

2 prepare the cake

Remove the frosting decorations from the sheet cake and trim the cake board (see pages 14 and 15). Put the cake, on its trimmed board, on a 13 × 19-inch cake board and attach with glue.

In a medium bowl, stir 1 cup plus 2 tablespoons of chocolate frosting until smooth. Frost the cake with a small offset spatula. Dip the spatula in hot water, shake off the excess, and smooth the frosting. Clean up the board and refrigerate the cake.

3 make the eyeballs

Dust a work surface with cornstarch. Roll out a green Tootsie Fruit Roll. Using the mouth of a dry empty plastic water bottle, stamp out 4 circles, pressing firmly while twisting. Using a #4 round paintbrush, brush the circles with water and then attach them to 4 gumballs. Tint a vanilla Tootsie Fruit Roll blue with 2 drops blue liquid food coloring, kneading in 1 drop at a time. Roll it out, stamp out 4 blue rounds, and attach them to the remaining 4 gumballs. Set the eyeballs aside in an area dusted with cornstarch, not letting them touch.

4 shape the head

Lightly trim the top of the pound cake to make it flat. Reduce its length to 9 inches by cutting equal amounts off each end. Put the cake horizontally on a work surface. Cut the cake into one 5-inch piece and one 4-inch piece. Reorient the 4-inch piece vertically, center it in front of the 5-inch piece, and attach it with chocolate frosting.

At the top left and right corners of the head, measure in ¾ inch diagonally toward the center of the cake and cut off the corners. To form the cheekbones, relocate the 2 cut-off corners directly under the 5-inch piece, on either side of the 4-inch piece with the corners facing out, as shown in the diagram. Attach with frosting.

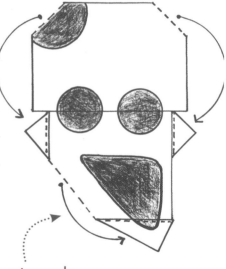

cut your cake like this

Measure 1½ inches from the bottom left corner of the head and make a mark. Line up a knife angled between the mark and the bottom of the left cheekbone and slice through. Slide the piece around to the bottom of the cake, pointed side down, to form the chin. Attach with frosting.

The cake should now resemble the zombie head shown in the diagram. Using your fingers and thumbs, press down lightly into the cake to create the cavities (shown in gray) for 2 eye sockets, one for the mouth, and another for an exposed area of the brain.

5 place and frost the head

Put the sheet cake vertically on a work surface. Using your hand and an offset spatula, lift the zombie head onto the sheet cake, flush with the top. In a bowl, tint 1 cup vanilla frosting gray using black food coloring. Frost the head. Don't worry about crumbs in the frosting because another layer will be applied over it. Refrigerate until firm, 15 to 20 minutes.

In a small bowl, mix ½ cup vanilla frosting with 16 drops green, 1 drop red, and 5 yellow drops liquid food coloring. In a separate bowl, tint ¼ cup vanilla frosting black.

Using a 1-inch paintbrush, loosely apply the green frosting to the cake to resemble decayed flesh, letting parts of the gray frosting show through. Using a ½-inch paintbrush, apply black frosting to the insides of the eye sockets and the mouth.

6 make the oozing brain

In a bowl, mix three quarters of an individual vanilla pudding cup with ¼ cup of the cooked macaroni and 4 drops of liquid red food coloring, creating a rose color. Spoon the brain mixture onto the head as shown in the photo. Use the ½-inch paintbrush to apply some of the red pudding mixture randomly on the face over the green frosting.

7 decorate the face

In the mouth, press the Trident White gum pieces into the cake to make the teeth, 3 on the top and 2 on the bottom.

Fill a zip-top plastic bag with the black frosting and cut ¼ inch off the tip. Pipe the frosting around the eye sockets and the mouth, and make 2 teardrop openings for the nose and 2 piped lines for the right cheek.

Scatter the Big League Chew as the hair, letting it flow over the sheet cake and onto the board. In a small bowl, stir ¼ cup vanilla frosting until smooth; spoon it into a plastic bag and cut ⅛ inch off the tip. In another bowl, tint ¼ cup vanilla frosting black; fill a plastic bag with the frosting and cut ⅛ inch off the tip. Pipe black squiggle lines all over the hair, and repeat with vanilla frosting squiggles over the black.

Remove a strand from the Twizzlers Pull 'n' Peel and cut three 3-inch pieces. Insert them into the left eye socket. Cut one 4-inch piece and put it under the right eye socket. Stir the Jell-O to form chunks, and spoon small amounts into the mouth, the left eye socket, and the brain. Sprinkle a few pieces of the cooked macaroni in the mouth and add a small amount of the remaining oozing brain mixture. Drape 2 gummi worms from the mouth.

Put a green eyeball in the right eye socket and a blue eyeball on the left cheek. With the black frosting bag used for the hair, pipe a dot in each pupil and a line around the iris.

8 finish the cake

Using an offset spatula, smear chocolate frosting on the board around the sheet cake. Sprinkle Oreo cookie crumbs over the sheet cake and press them into the sides, letting whatever falls remain. Scatter the remaining gummi worms, macaroni, and chunks of Jell-O around the cake. Arrange the remaining eyeballs around the sides. Then pipe the iris and pupil on each eyeball with black frosting.

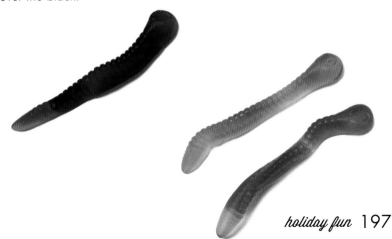

dreidel

When designing the Hanukkah cake, Rick considered many symbolic objects used to celebrate the holiday and decided on making a dreidel. He liked the look of the four-sided toy, and included the *Gimmel* letter on top of the dreidel and chocolate coins for the *gelt*. The dreidel is made as a dimensional piece lying on a sheet cake, versus cutting out a shape from the sheet cake, as we felt it gave the most realistic appearance. When grouping the chocolate coins together, try to alternate the sides so different scenes are showing.

SERVES 20 TO 25

LEVEL OF DIFFICULTY: 1.5

special tools

1 (9 × 13-inch) cake board

Small offset spatula

1 (10-inch) cardboard cake circle

1 (10-inch) wooden skewer

Wire cutters

ingredients

1 (8 × 12-inch) sheet cake (¼ sheet) with vanilla frosting

3 cups vanilla frosting (2 16-ounce cans)

1 (10.75-ounce) frozen pound cake (we use Sara Lee), thawed

1 Little Debbie Swiss Roll

Paste or gel paste food coloring: blue (SEE SOURCES, PAGE 201)

12 blue Twizzlers Rainbow Twists (from 3 12.4-ounce packages)

16 chocolate gold coins

1 prepare the cake

Remove the frosting decorations from the sheet cake and trim the cake board (see pages 14 and 15). Put the cake, on its trimmed board, on a 9 × 13-inch cake board and attach with glue.

In a medium bowl, stir 1½ cups vanilla frosting until smooth. Using an offset spatula, frost the cake. Dip the spatula in hot water, shake off the excess, and carefully smooth the frosting. Clean up the board and refrigerate the cake.

2 make the dreidel

Lightly trim the top of the pound cake to make it flat, and remove the side crusts. Put the cake down vertically on a work surface. Measure 4 inches from the top edge and score a line across the cake. Score a second line 1½ inches below the first line. Cut through the second line, making a 5½-inch-long loaf. Discard the trimmings

Flip the cake on its side with the scored line facing you on the right. Line up a knife on the top surface between the beginning of the scored line and the top right corner on the same surface. Cut down following the scored line, and discard the corner.

Put the cake down vertically with the wedge facing you. Find the center point on the bottom edge. Line up the knife between the center point and the left edge of the scored line, and cut through. Repeat on the right side of the cake. Discard the trimmings. Put the cake on a 10-inch cardboard cake circle.

3 make the dreidel handle

Attach the Little Debbie Swiss Roll to the center of the top of the pound cake. Cut a 10-inch skewer in half, using wire cutters. Push the pointed end of the skewer through the Swiss Roll and into the pound cake.

4 frost the dreidel

In a bowl, tint ¾ cup vanilla frosting a medium blue. Scoop 2 tablespoons into a separate bowl for crumb-coating. Using an offset spatula, crumb-coat the cake with a light layer of blue frosting. Clean up the cake circle and refrigerate until firm, about 15 minutes.

Frost the cake blue, and smooth the frosting. Clean up the cardboard and refrigerate until firm, 20 to 25 minutes.

Take both cakes out of the refrigerator. Using your hand and an offset spatula, center the dreidel on top of the sheet cake.

5 make the hebrew letter

In a bowl, tint 2 tablespoons frosting a light blue. Spoon it into a zip-top plastic bag and cut ⅛ inch off the tip. On top of the dreidel, pipe the outline of the *Gimmel* letter. Fill in the outline by piping thin horizontal lines back and forth, and carefully smooth the frosting.

6 finish the cake

Mix all the remaining blue frosting (without crumbs) together. Tint ¼ cup of the frosting dark blue by adding more blue food coloring. Scoop it into a zip-top plastic bag and cut ⅛ inch off the tip. Pipe a border around all edges of the dreidel, including the top of the handle and the base where it meets the body, and around the *Gimmel* letter.

Make top and bottom borders around the cake with blue Twizzlers, cutting with scissors to fit. Arrange the gold coins on the cake in groups, as shown.

sources

Some of the best sources for buying candies are the least obvious. Check convenience stores, party supply stores, drugstores, dollar stores, and even video rental stores. Amazon.com has an excellent selection of bulk candies for purchase. Also, many candy companies have online ordering and/or information on finding a product locally.

bakeware and cake decorating supply stores

Beryl's Cake Decorating and Pastry Supplies
www.beryls.com
P.O. Box 1584
North Springfield, VA 22151
Phone: (800) 488-2749

Country Kitchen SweetArt
www.countrykitchensa.com
4621 Speedway Drive
Fort Wayne, IN 46825
Phone: (800) 497-3927

Global Sugar Art
www.globalsugarart.com
Phone: (800) 420-6088

Gloria's Cake and Candy Supplies
www.gloriascakecandysuplys.com
12453 Washington Boulevard
West Los Angeles, CA 90066
Phone: (310) 391-4557

Kerekes Bakery & Restaurant Equipment
www.bakedeco.com
6103 15th Avenue
Brooklyn, NY 11219
Phone: (800) 525-5556

New York Cake and Baking Distributor
www.nycake.com
56 West 22nd Street
New York, NY 10010
Phone: (800) 942-2539

Sugarcraft
www.sugarcraft.com
3665 Dixie Highway
Hamilton, OH 45015
Phone: (513) 896-7089

Sur La Table
www.surlatable.com
Locations throughout the
United States
Phone: (800) 243-0852

Williams-Sonoma
www.williams-sonoma.com
Locations throughout the
United States
Phone: (877) 812-6235

Wilton Industries
www.wilton.com
Phone: (888) 373-4588

candy stores

Candy Warehouse
www.candywarehouse.com
Phone: (310) 343-4099

Dylan's Candy Bar
www.dylanscandybar.com
Locations throughout the
United States
Phone: (866) 939-5267

Hometown Favorites
www.hometownfavorites.com
Phone: (888) 694-2656

Sweet Factory
www.sweetfactory.com
Locations throughout the
United States
Phone: (877) 817-9338

craft and party supply stores

Jo-Ann Fabric and Craft Stores
www.joann.com
Locations throughout the
United States
Phone: (888) 739-4120

Michael's Stores
www.michaels.com
Locations throughout the
United States
Phone: (800) 642-4235

Party City
www.partycity.com
Locations throughout the
United States
Phone: (800) 727-8924

boxes and packaging

Asian Ideas
www.asianideas.com
Phone: (877) 407-9259

Paper Mart
www.papermart.com
2164 North Batavia Street
Orange, CA 92865
Phone: (800) 745-8800

acknowledgments

We will never look at a cookbook the same way again.

When we started our literary journey, we didn't realize the incredible time commitment a cookbook requires on the part of its authors and another whole team of people. Besides designing cakes and writing the text, there is the testing, photography, illustrations, art design, editing, printing, and promotion of the book, and this all happens before the book is even released. We are grateful to the many individuals who have dedicated their support, creativity, guidance, and time to be a part of this very special project.

To Holly Schmidt and Allan Penn, our wonderful agents, for all their hard work, encouragement, and belief in us.

To our fabulous editor at Clarkson Potter, Ashley Phillips, for being passionate about our book from day one and for giving us flawless editing and endless support. You magically knew how to guide us without stifling our creativity.

To the entire team at Clarkson Potter: Rica Allannic, for giving us an opportunity we never dreamed possible. Jane Treuhaft, for treating our store-bought candies and frostings like they were foie gras and truffles, and for spending so much time with us. Your creative vision inspired us to put our best foot forward. Also to Pam Krauss, Doris Cooper, Patricia Shaw, Ashley Tucker, Philip Leung, Carly Gorga, Donna Passannante, and Sean Boyles.

To our photographer, Ryan Siphers, for bringing the cakes and ingredients to life with your amazing photos and styling. Thank you for devoting so much time and attention to our "secret" project and leaving your beautiful island to come play on ours.

To our A-Team—Joan and George Reichart, Dee Applebee, Nicki Yamane, Beth Stephens, Anita Reyes, Paul Powell, Lauren Reichart, Bill Reichart, Emmy Reichart, Brenna Reichart, Maya Yamane, and Christie Nix—for making sure all our ducks were in a row. We couldn't have done it without your hard work and we owe a huge debt of gratitude to each of you.

To our wonderful clients, the media, and Rick's awesome hosts and students around the world, for singing our praises and supporting cakelava over the years. To our followers and friends on Facebook and Twitter, and to the readers of our blog: your comments and kind words are something we look forward to every day.

To our mentors: Elin Katz, Joan Spitler, Anne Welch, Kari Von Wening, Jodie Chase, Jan Birnbaum, and Jonathan Sundstrom. Your guidance and expertise gave us the confidence to pursue our passions.

To Food Network, the High Noon Denver team, and Megan Garafola and her crew: you believed in us and made life more exciting.

To our extended families—aunts, uncles, cousins, stepfamilies, close friends (you know who you are), and colleagues in the cake and wedding industries. We are lucky to have such an amazing group of people in our lives. You always supported our endeavors and understood our crazy schedules.

To our siblings Bill, Andrew, and Lauren: you brighten our lives and push us to do our very best.

To Kazuo Y., a grandfather, an inspirational businessman, and a war hero: we wish we could have shared our book with you and Mary.

To Linda H., our third mother, for unconditionally supporting us through our best and worst times.

To Tony, Margaret, Miranda, Adam, Eric, Annie, Laura, and David: you have been part of our most special (and the craziest) times of our lives and have always been there for us.

Finally, to our parents: George, Joan, Linda, and Deane: You all gave us a strong foundation and the confidence to take on this crazy challenge. You helped make us who we are today and we are forever grateful!

index

about the authors

Rick and Sasha Reichart are the owners of cakelava, an innovative cake design company located in Kailua, Oahu, Hawaii. Rick and his designs have been featured on *Food Network Challenge*, in *People*, and in numerous national and international wedding and cake-industry publications. Rick frequently teaches at events around the world. Visit their websites at extremecakeovers.com and cakelava.com.